WELCOME HOME
RASPBERRY
THE LUCKY ONES

These three plays, written by the winner of *Dra*
Award for 1982, testify to the topicality and ver:

Welcome Home, a 'blistering, exhausting study (
Paras recently returned from the Falklands War uncovers a gaping wound in our
society's moral carapace and sets leeches, not balm, to the sores. The result is
painful and unforgettable . . . Marchant creates a nerve-wracking world which
always threatens to topple into nightmare, as one after another of the survivors
crack, unable to rationalise and find meaning in their comrade's death . . .
Marchant has seen that the deeper significance of the war lay not in any military
lessons or victory but in the ease with which certain ideas and moral codes –
thought to have withered away with the end of Empire – were called back to vivid,
phantasmagoric life.' Michael Stewart, *Tribune*

Raspberry is set in a hospital ward where two women, one a seventeen year old
about to have an abortion, the other a thirty year old facing an operation to 'cure'
her infertility, are drawn together by their shared sense of shame, failure and,
utimately, defiance. 'Intensely moving, an extraordinary achievement for a male
writer' Rosemary Say, *Sunday Telegraph* 'This is surely the most convincing piece
of writing a man could ever produce about women.' David Roper, *Event*

The Lucky Ones is 'riotously amusing and highly subversive . . . Tony Marchant,
already earmarked as one of the most promising young playwrights around,
comes of age with a vengeance. In a basement over-flowing with boxes and files,
four young clerks at a firm of stockbrokers, trapped in an endless round of
mindless drudgery, reveal their true selves in a mounting spiral of vividly written
arguments and escapades . . . Marchant's dazzling observations on the petty
restrictions and humiliations imposed by employers on those at the bottom of the
heap are steeped in acid.' Malcolm Hay, *Time Out*

WELCOME HOME

RASPBERRY

THE LUCKY ONES

Three Plays by
TONY MARCHANT

A Methuen New Theatrescript
Methuen · London

For Adrian

A METHUEN PAPERBACK

First published as a Methuen Paperback original in 1983 by Methuen London Ltd,
11 New Fetter Lane, London EC4P 4EE

Copyright © 1983 by Tony Marchant

ISBN 0 413 53820 6

WELCOME HOME

Welcome Home was first presented by Paines Plough on 8 February 1983 at the Old Town Hall Arts Centre, Hemel Hempstead, with the following cast:

POLO	Tony London
DENIS	Garry Olsen
WALTERS	Mark Wingett
GOLDY	Ian Mercer
SHARP	Robert Pugh
FISHER	Michael Townsend

Directed by John Chapman
Designed by Caroline Beaver
Lighting by Tim Speechley

The production was subsequently toured by Paines Plough and opened at the Royal Court Theatre Upstairs on 16 March 1983.

DENIS, POLO *and* WALTERS *are in a railway waiting-room. Not in uniform but with kitbags and grey cover cases for their uniforms. Long silence before anything is said.*

POLO: What time's the train?

DENIS: Forty-three minutes past.

WALTERS: Seventeen minutes to.

POLO: They're late.

DENIS: They'll be here.

WALTERS: I uncoupled a train once – me and a mate climbed over the fence of this depot. One o'clock in the morning. Train was in the sidings, like. This mate of mine – he's in the engineers, headcase he is – about thirty fucking seconds it took him. Train was supposed to have eight carriages – it only had five when we'd finished with it – or three like – depending on which end the driver's cab was. Couldn't see in the dark. Right laugh.

POLO: What's the time now?

WALTERS: If the big hand is on twenty and the little hand is on two, then it must be, then it must be . . . what time must it be Polo?

POLO: Five to three. Or twenty five past nine – depending on which end the driver's cab is. Can't see in the dark. Right laugh.

WALTERS: Watch yourself Polo.

POLO: I never do anything else Walters.

DENIS: Pack it in you two.

POLO: I've got a packet in. A packet in here. (*Producing a pack of Polo Mints.*) Anyone want one?

WALTERS: You're fucking screwy, you.

DENIS: You ever been to the house before Polo, like when you was on leave with him?

POLO: No. Never been.

WALTERS: You couldn't take him anywhere. He shits in the bidet, this boy.

POLO: Goldy's been.

DENIS: Best mates. (*Pause.*) I'll be glad when it's all over.

WALTERS: What – so you can forget about it?

DENIS (*darkening*): I didn't mean it that way, all right. (*Pause.*) I was glad to be asked. But we're not going to be judging marrows at a fucking garden fete.

Pause.

WALTERS: We'll be there to do him justice. Give him what he deserves. Right Polo?

POLO: Have you heard the new Number One – it's the Jam. Came straight in from nowhere. That's the third time they've done that. *Going Underground, Town Called Malice* and now *Beat Surrender.* They're the only group that's ever done that – apart from Slade. Them and Slade. (*Pause.*) They're late.

WALTERS (*noticing some graffiti on the wall*): Here, look at this, look. 'Chipping Sodbury bootboys rule OK?' Is that a joke or what?

DENIS: What d'you think? Mind you, I did meet a skinhead once called Nigel.

POLO: And I know a wanker called Roger.

WALTERS: Watch yourself Polo.

POLO: I never do anything else Roger.

WALTERS: I'm warning ya.

DENIS: Leave it out for fuck's sake.

POLO: Shouldn't be slagging each other . . . we're a team . . . working for each other . . . winning team . . .

WALTERS: There's another one here – 'Arsenal Northbank fear no one'. Jokers. Fucking skinheads, bootboys – what do they know? A kick and a punch from behind – on the terraces – three onto one, mugging old ladies in the dark, throwing stones through pakis' windows and they think they're hard. They don't know what it's all about. When you've done two tours of duty and fought in a war 8,000 miles across the world, then you're due for a bit of respect. They'd be shitting bricks – all they can do is swear and clench their fists at other lads. They're not fit to wipe my nose. I'm worth ten of them. They don't know what hard is. They've got no idea.

Pause.

Notice how no one else comes in here. Everywhere we go we take over, take control. That's how it must seem to those poor fuckers having to sit out there on the benches shivering.

POLO: They're going to miss the train. Then we'll all be fucked.

DENIS: There'll be other trains.

POLO: Well I wish they'd fucking hurry up. We should all be going down together.

DENIS: All the lads together.

POLO: The party. (*Pause.*) Here – how d'you stop a marine from drowning?

DENIS: Take your foot off his head.

POLO: Heard about the Irishman who thought masturbation was what you put in tomato soup.

DENIS: I don't get it.

POLO: Nor do I.

DENIS: What you up to Walters?

WALTERS (*writing some graffiti on the wall*): 'Ready for Anything' and the crest. This is something worth putting on the wall. This means something.

POLO: You're still a vandal in the eyes of the law. (*Pause.*) Uncoupling trains, scratching on waiting-room walls – what's . . . what's British Rail ever done to you eh?

WALTERS: Either of you two got a blue pen? Bring it up better like.

GOLDY *comes in.*

GOLDY: All right.

WALTERS: About bloody time. Where's Ian?

GOLDY: How the fuck do I know? We might have gone on leave at the same time but we didn't go off and book the honeymoon suite at the Dorchester. Much as I like, admire and respect our corp and try to follow the fine example he sets, I'm not married to the fucker.

POLO: How was it – all right?

GOLDY: Not too bad. Bit preoccupied like, y'know.

DENIS: Flash? (*Offering him a cigarette.*)

GOLDY: Ta, Den.

DENIS: Did you go and have your curry?

GOLDY (*smiling*): Yeah. I could eat chicken massala till it comes out of me ear.

WALTERS: The only fucking curry I've ever had came straight out of me arse.

POLO (*to* WALTERS): I'm surprised you've ever been in one, cos where you come from you think you're being adventurous eating smokey bacon crisps.

GOLDY: Train's about five minutes innit?

WALTERS: Seventeen to.

GOLDY: What are you – the speaking clock?

WALTERS: Precision Goldy. S'what helps make a good soldier. Precision is the most exquisite fruit . . .

GOLDY: And favourite son of discipline.

POLO: You better watch out Goldy – he's been saying how hard he is . . . respect . . . you gotta respect him.

WALTERS: I was talking about all of us pratt, all of us – what we've been through . . . compared to other lads. What we've done. Even among other soldiers, craphat.

GOLDY (*dryly*): We're special. We're cherry berets.

WALTERS: And everyone knows it.

DENIS: He still believes everything Grin told him like they was extracts from the Bible or something.

GOLDY (*pause*): You will be faster than a speeding train, you will leap buildings at a single bound, you will have X-ray vision, bullets will bounce off your bodies. In other words you will become supermen. In other words you will become paras. You will not, I am sorry to say, get to wear a cloak nor will you quite learn how to fly but I can promise you this – you will have no fear of Kryptonite. (*Pause.*) How we laughed.

WALTERS: I'd rather be a Kilgore. A warry fucker. Or like that sergeant in 3rd who licked the blood off his bayonet after he'd stuck it in. Licked it clean. A real warry bastard him. He'd heard that's what they did in Vietnam.

POLO: Grin made me do four circuits round the Spoon once . . . with me pack – for lack of application. Your bondook's a cunt of a thing if your fingers are numb with cold. Mine were. He never liked me. You don't say.

Pause.

DENIS: Nice shirt you've got on there, Goldy.

GOLDY: Girlfriend bought it for me. You know how they like to make a fuss when you go back – she says she likes the idea of not seeing me for a fair while – so that we can have one of those reunions like they do in films like – you now, run into each others' arms from forty paces, kisses that last about an hour and a half. Holding hands all the time, being all over each other and then the sweet sorrow of parting again. The tears. She says it makes the relationship seem more exciting, more intense. Anything normal would be an anti-climax she reckons. She's read too many books, that's her trouble. I feel like fucking Heathcliffe on the moors sometimes.

DENIS: More like Lassie come home I would have thought.

POLO: Here – what's Heathcliffe?

DENIS: Who's Heathcliffe.

GOLDY: Ain't you ever heard of *Wuthering Heights* you thick prick? Heathcliffe and Cathy. It was a book.

POLO: Kate Bush – *Wuthering Heights*. The song.

GOLDY: They made a film of it as well.

POLO: What – a musical?

GOLDY: Fucking hell!

POLO: March 1978 it got to Number One – debut single and after that in April, Boney M had the new Number One. *By the Rivers of Babylon* and *Brown Girl in the Ring* – double A side. In the charts for forty weeks altogether it was – fantastic innit?

GOLDY: I'm sorry about that Wally – I should never have brought that bit of culture into the conversation. Let's talk about knobbing birds up against walls.

WALTERS: Funny you should say that – did I tell you about the other night . . .

POLO: Oh shut up Walters, you dirty bastard. You're diseased, you've got more sores than you have skin. If I was a bird I wouldn't go near you unless I was wearing an asbestos suit. You're the man who invented herpes.

WALTERS: And you've worn away the palms of your hands, because you want so much. You'll never be able to get your fortune told, you've rubbed all the lines away.

GOLDY (*looking at the graffiti*): Who did this?

WALTERS: Me.

GOLDY: That's defacing public property, you know that don't you?

SHARP *appears at the doorway.*

SHARP: Not defacing, embellishing Goldy. You should know that. Decorating, dignifying, enlivening, transmogrifying even – that's a long word innit? But more than all that saying: we have been here and we are proud. We are proud of who we are. Fear us. Respect us. Are we ready to get our arses on the train now then? We don't want to miss it do we? Punctuality is a practice of precision which as you know is the most exquisite fruit and favourite son of discipline. Right Polo?

POLO: Definitely

SHARP: Very fucking definitely. Come on then.

The five on a train in a compartment.
SHARP *is combing his hair in front of the mirror.*

SHARP: Clickety-clack. Clickety-clack.

GOLDY: Didn't know you did impersonations Ian.

SHARP: I'm a very talented person Goldy. I'm an all-round entertainer. Half of my real potential hasn't ever been brought out into the open. Lack of opportunity I suppose. But I'm not bitter – no, not me. Because when all is said and done my son, I've proved myself. At home and abroad. I have proved myself.

POLO: Sounds . . . sounds a bit like machine-gun . . . firing sounds . . .

DENIS: What?

POLO: N-noise of the train going across the tracks.

WALTERS: Which one – sub, light, heavy or general purpose gun, Polo?

SHARP: Now, now don't take the urine

Wally – Polo's just had a very poetic thought. Highly poetic. Not many soldiers, not many people could have come up with a thought like that, could have that kind of imagination. Another case of undetected talent there I reckon, just like what I've got. Potential. I think I'm going to write down what you just said Polo. That's worth remembering that is.

POLO: Fuck off Ian – do us a favour.

WALTERS: That's not very poetic is it?

POLO: I'll fucking do you Walters. I mean it.

SHARP: We can do without that kind of talk, Polo. What if a nice old lady overheard that kind of talk, or a scoutmaster or Mr and Mrs General Public – what then eh? Our reputations would be tarnished, well and truly shop soiled. Is that what you want?

GOLDY: Especially as we're sitting in a first class compartment. With second class tickets.

SHARP: You complaining then Goldy?

GOLDY: Not me. I never complain.

SHARP: Then what's your problem private?

GOLDY: My problem?

WALTERS: Perhaps it's his fucking conscience, eh?

DENIS: Here, Ian – what would happen to our reputations if there's a ticket inspector on this train and he wants to look at our tickets and he tells us to go back to the other carriage – what do we do then? – troop off like naughty boys and get made to look like a bunch of twats who tried to fiddle British Rail or stay and argue it out and get made to look like a bunch of thugs who happen to be soldiers?

SHARP: We do neither, Denis. I don't think there's going to be any problem you see. No problem at all. And why do you think I say that? – because I'm the corp and I have to keep things, you lot ticking over and feeling happy? No. Because it wouldn't do for me to have doubts or a negative attitude, because I set an example? No again. Because I'm a fucking cocky bastard? No no, no.

DENIS: You going to let us in on the secret then?

SHARP: It's no secret Denis. The reason why I say we'll have no problem is on account of how I see the ordinary British man. The ordinary British ticket collector. His gratitude, his appreciation. For what we did not so long ago. He won't have forgotten what happened and he might even be an ex-soldier himself. Don't worry about it lads, he'll say – put your feet up, I'll get the steward in to bring some coffee and biscuits – on the house.

DENIS: And a free film show and five foot stools. Jimmy Saville ain't mentioned nothing about this.

SHARP: I'll tell you something – my scoring rate has gone up ten times in the past few months. Not that I had any trouble before. But I've only got to walk into a place in uniform with me beret on and I get admiring glances, pats on the back, smiles and nods. People offering to buy me drinks. Even when I'm wearing me V-neck and jeans, I've only got to mention that I was in the South Atlantic and the birds start slipping me their telephone numbers, they can't wait to put their tongues in me ear, their hands down me flies, their tits in me face. Course, my cock is always happy to salute, go on manoeuvres, load and fire. It's like being Adam Ant and Roy of the Rovers rolled into one. Don't knock it, that's what I say.

WALTERS: I get a lot of that as well.

Pause.

GOLDY: I can understand it though, can't you? I mean, what it did for our image like. We was righting wrongs, we came to the rescue.

SHARP: Bit like Superman.

DENIS (*not really sure what's going on*): You shall have no fear of Kryptonite.

GOLDY: Point is though – when people see us now – the comfortable, civilised, filling in their pools coupon, silent, spineless majority – when they see us now – we're not just soldiers . . . we're something more. And it's more than just admiration, it's . . . hope. (*Pause.*) Don't you reckon, corp?

SHARP (*cagey*): Capturing the imagination it's called.

GOLDY: The timid and the disillusioned fucking sheep – waiting for a new mood to sweep the country, to have real fucking values again.

SHARP: Yeah.

GOLDY: And we're the boys to have made that happen. We're a nation again. That's right innit?

SHARP: Why not. Anyway, what I'm saying is – ticket collector'll be all right, don't worry about that. He'll say we deserve 1st class. He'll see.

GOLDY: Let's hope so.

DENIS: Be nice if it applied on buses as well.

WALTERS: If your bottle's gone Goldy – you can always go and sit in the fucking luggage compartment.

GOLDY: What? And miss the pleasure of your company? It's like asking Prince Charles to stop playing polo.

POLO: What?

WALTERS: Nothing to do with you.

POLO: Are we going through any tunnels d'you know . . . any tunnels coming up? Bulbs are out – look.

DENIS: First class travel and no lights in the carriage – what a rip off.

SHARP: What you worried about Polo? I hope you're not going to try and molest anyone in the dark are you? I hope you're going to keep your hands to yourself. You know the regiment takes a very dim view of anyone who can't keep his hands to himself. Except when it comes to the old slags who drink in the Red Deer or any other pub in the town where the old slags hang out. Then you can or rather you're expected to put your hands wherever they will go – and other bits of your anatomy as well. Anyone not attempting to do so gets strong doubts cast about his . . . pedigree. His . . . er . . . leanings.

POLO: No tunnels is there Goldy?

GOLDY: Not that I can remember, no.

POLO: Right.

Pause.

SHARP: Clickety-clack. Clickety-clack. I like travelling on trains – you get to see a bit of the old scenery don't ya? Nature. I like a bit of greenery. (*Pause.*) What's the most important thing we have to do tomorrow – Denis?

DENIS: Trust each other.

SHARP: Tout.

ALL: Trust each other.

SHARP: Didn't quite catch that Goldy.

GOLDY: Trust each other.

SHARP: Fox is coming down to read the message.

Pause.

We all feel the loss of our mates – not just Terry but all the others as well. You'll be entitled to feel choked up tomorrow, there'd be something wrong with you if you didn't. (*Pause.*) But you know as well as I do that we're going down there to do a job as well, whether you like it or not – people are going to be watching and we're going to prove we're as good as advertised on TV – aren't we chaps? I've heard that when they bring the new action man out he'll be wearing a red beret. He'll be one of us. But he'll have to learn to sleep with his eyes open – like we do.

WALTERS: And shave with a broken bottle – like we do.

SHARP: Don't get fucking clever.

POLO: Anyone mind if I switch me cassette on? It's the Top Thirty. I recorded it. Guess what's Number One? Better not have it on too loud eh? Madness have gone down to Number Six this week.

DENIS: Anyone want anything from the buffet?

GOLDY: Get us a coffee and a sandwich will ya?

WALTERS: I'll have a beer please, Denis.

DENIS: Corp?

SHARP (*producing his hip flask*): It's all right – I'm self-sufficient.

DENIS: Polo? Polo! Tap him for us will ya.

POLO: What?

DENIS: I'm going to the buffet.

POLO: No thanks – I got these. (*A packet of Polos.*)

Pause.

WALTERS (*indicating the cassette*): That's not very suitable for where we're going is it?

POLO: I won't be playing it will I?

WALTERS: Be a shame if the batteries for it got nicked wouldn't it?

POLO: I'd go and buy some more.

WALTERS: Be an even bigger shame if it got accidentally knocked over and smashed to pieces.

POLO: Don't pick your nose Walters or your brain'll cave in.

WALTERS: D'you remember that time when you was supposed to be on guard duty Polo, and Grin caught you listening to that in your room instead. Tell us what he made you do.

POLO: He made me dance to it. He made me dance to the records it was playing. In the middle of the parade ground.

WALTERS: Cracks me up to think about it.

POLO: I'll crack you up one day.

WALTERS: One shot.

POLO: Two shots is pussy.

WALTERS: This is this.

POLO (*gun to head*): Click.

SHARP: I find train journeys very relaxing. (*No response.*)

POLO: How . . . how long? Till we get there?

GOLDY: About another ten-fifteen minutes.

POLO: Me brother's taping the new ABC LP for me. *Lexicon of Love.* He bought it last week. Says it's really good.

GOLDY: I've only heard the singles.

DENIS *re-enters.*

DENIS: Light refreshments.

Darkness.

POLO: Thought you said there was no tunnels Goldy! No tunnels you said!

Turning the cassette up very loud.

Front room. The five soldiers. A coffin, mounted on a table. They are holding plates of food.

WALTERS: Dirty spic bastards.

DENIS: His mum looks as though she could do with a few years sleep.

GOLDY: She's been on tranquillisers for months. Record year for drug companies this is.

DENIS: What d'you mean?

GOLDY: Profits. Terry's mum has become one of their major investors. Consumer of the year, like. Her prize is valium for life. (*Pause.*) We remind her of him.

POLO: Nice coffin.

WALTERS (*incredulous*): What?

POLO: Beautiful coffin. N-nice wood.

DENIS: Stupid sod.

GOLDY: Pity we ain't got a camera with us. Could have took a team photo – us five kneeling in front of it – arms folded, smiling. Like when you win the FA Cup.

WALTERS: Was that supposed to be funny?

GOLDY: That's his souvenir – we've got our warry photos. He's got that.

SHARP: It's better than being left in the mass grave at Ajax Bay – at least he'll be able to have a decent ceremony now – honoured in the proper way. A soldier's funeral. His family wanted him brought home.

DENIS: They'll have a grave to visit now. Somewhere to put flowers, kneel down, say prayers and all that. Get an headstone put up. At least he's with 'em now.

GOLDY: In the flesh.

DENIS: That's a bit out of order.

GOLDY: Fatality's a funny word innit – sounds like the name of an Italian ice-cream don't it? Vanilla flavour fatality. Boys and men with the life blown out of 'em. That's a bit . . . what's the word . . . over explicit like.

SHARP: It was a war – people, soldiers got killed like in other wars. It's a fact of life, a fact of war. There's no getting away from it.

GOLDY: It's inevitable. That's another great word innit? Inevitable. Fucking inevitable.

SHARP: That's enough. Keep your mouth shut. Remember where you are. Remember where you are.

POLO: Does anyone want my coleslaw?

WALTERS: No sense of occasion you, have you?

POLO: I was only asking if anyone wanted . . .

DENIS: S'funny – something like that being in a room like this. It don't go . . . don't fit. Everything else in here is so normal. Television, settee, bowl of fruit. S'hard to match them together.

GOLDY: Especially when you know who's inside it. And you know that really . . .

POLO: *Top of the Pops* is on later.

SHARP: Be draped in the Union Jack tomorrow. With his beret.

WALTERS: Is Fisher still going to bear?

SHARP: He'll be here tomorrow.

POLO: There's a jukebox in that pub down the road. Anyone . . . anyone got any tens? For afterwards. What about QPR – walking away with it in the second division ain't they? I put it down to their new playing surface. They've got a really good home record. This is the first proper funeral I've ever been to. There's nowhere to put me coleslaw.

Pause.

SHARP: Had some bottle that day eh? Unbelievable. Half a battery, three guns and two mortars against a battalion of 1500. And we zapped the fuckers.

WALTERS: Best. Live the Cav in Vietnam.

GOLDY: Terry had a rabbit's foot tucked in one of his boots.

DENIS: There was so many St Christophers being carried around, anyone'd think we was going on a pilgrimage. Till we got there anyway.

SHARP: Prince Charles is supposed to have sent a personal message of condolence to his mum and dad. D'you think that sounds likely?

POLO: He shook my hand at Brize Norton. Said well done. He didn't have a chance to speak to me when he came to Aldershot for the memorial service. Ask me how I was getting on, like.

WALTERS: Listen to him. Since he got his campaign medal he thinks he's a bloody celebrity now.

DENIS: I thought he was pissed off because it weren't the VC. He thought they'd given him the wrong one by mistake.

SHARP: No, they went to the right people all right.

Pause.

WALTERS: Will there by hymns tomorrow?

GOLDY: No, they'll be playing *The Wombles of Wimbledon Common* followed by *We All Live in a Yellow Submarine.*

POLO: Funny choice of music innit?

SHARP: There'll be one or two hymns Wally.

WALTERS: I used to be an altar boy. Me mum used to make me go to church when I was a little boy.

DENIS: Me too. I used to do the offertory.

SHARP: What's this – *Stars on Sunday*?

WALTERS: We used to nick the eucharist, put 'em in a bag with salt and vinegar and make out they were Golden Wonder crisps.

DENIS: I used to get right nervous taking the stuff up to the priest. Felt like a magician's assistant.

POLO: Have you ever realised that God spelt backwards is Dog? Makes you think don't it?

GOLDY: You won't get to heaven saying things like that.

POLO: I'm in no hurry.

Pause.

DENIS: Gets very touristy in the summer I've heard.

GOLDY: What does?

DENIS: Heaven. (*Pause.*) Anyway, who wants to go to a place that's full of fucking Roman Catholics? That's if you believe in it in the first place.

WALTERS: Death can be worthwhile though, can't it? I mean, like Terry's. It's not as if he got run over by a car is it? He died for something good didn't he?

DENIS: D'you order it? (*To* GOLDY.)

SHARP: Order what? (*No response.*) Order what – chicken tikka from the Star of India, front row seats at the London Palladium – what?

GOLDY: Wreath.

SHARP: What wreath is this?

GOLDY (*quietly*): Oh, I'm going to a funeral tomorrow, didn't I say? I thought I'd get him a wreath – custom like, you know, like when people get married and you're invited, you bring a present – like a toaster or a whisk or an alarm clock – it's a similar thing here. Only he can't say thank you can he?

DENIS: Me and Goldy clubbed together.

SHARP: Why weren't we asked?

DENIS: It was just something we wanted to do – personal like.

SHARP: It would have been nice to have been asked. It would have been . . . thoughtful, considerate, polite. It would have been the decent thing. After all, we're supposed to be a team, team up, mates – carrying the coffin of our dead mate. Us three'll give you the money – shared between five instead of three. Get it? Shared. Get your money out you two.

WALTERS: How much does it come to?

GOLDY: Can we sort it out afterwards please. Can we?

Pause.

SHARP (*emphatic*): How much?

DENIS: Fifteen quid.

SHARP: Three quid a piece then, right. So we give you nine. Here's a fiver.

POLO: I've only got a pound and a ten pound note.

SHARP: Give us that pound and now you owe us two quid.

WALTERS: Here's five.

DENIS: Two back.

POLO: If I give you ten you can give us those two fives.

DENIS: What for – you still won't be able to give him his two.

POLO: How many ones have you got then?

GOLDY: Jesus Christ! This ain't the floor of the Stock Exchange is it? Is it?

Pause.

DENIS: Has he got a large family Goldy? A lot of relatives like?

GOLDY: Quite a few I think.

SHARP: Most of the people who live round here'll probably turn out. To pay tribute, acknowledge their debt. That's if they appreciate what courage is, what a bloody feat of heroism means. I wouldn't have thought that heroes are ten a penny round here would you? Not falling off the trees exactly. (*Pause.*) They'll be lots watching tomorrow all right.

POLO: D-did you know that Errol Brown of Hot Chocolate's favourite record is *Dock of the Bay* by Otis Redding? He's the most successful British singer/ songwriter since the Beatles. Seventeen consecutive hits in eleven years. *Take my Chances on You* is the latest.

DENIS: Nice garden they've got out there. Well kept. Rosebushes as well. Shit.

POLO: That's what you need with rosebushes.

SHARP: We'd . . . we'd better be off in a minute.

DENIS: Give the family a bit of privacy. (*Pause.*) His sister looks a lot like him.

WALTERS: All right ain't she?

SHARP: Everyone sure he knows what he's supposed to do tomorrow?

GOLDY: We could always do a trial run. Got all the props we need.

SHARP: What about a bit of respect eh? A bit of dignity. That's the last time I tell you – I mean it.

GOLDY: Sorry.

Pause.

POLO: They . . . they do pork scratchings in that pub.

WALTERS: Who said the art of conversation is dead?

GOLDY: Terry liked . . .

DENIS: I've gone off them. It's like those dry roasted peanuts. I couldn't get enough of 'em.

WALTERS: Will we be throwing dirt into the grave?

POLO: B-better go now, eh corp. L-leave the family in peace, like. In privacy.

GOLDY: I'd like to stay – on me own, just for a few minutes.

SHARP: We'll wait for you.

DENIS: Outside eh?

Pause.

SHARP: Course.

GOLDY: Why don't I see you in the pub?

SHARP: You asking or telling.

GOLDY: Telling.

DENIS: What d'you want?

GOLDY: What d'you mean?

DENIS: To drink.

GOLDY: Oh – get us a pint of lager will ya.

SHARP: Polo – take these plates back to the kitchen.

WALTERS: I wonder if there's any more sausage rolls left.

GOLDY: Why?

WALTERS: I think they're nice, that's all. I thought I might . . .

GOLDY: Is that all you think?

WALTERS: What d'you mean?

GOLDY: Nothing – doesn't matter.

DENIS: See you in a bit then.

GOLDY: Yeah.

Pause – no one leaves, nothing happens.

POLO: Shouldn't we . . . er . . . don't we have to c-cross ourselves, make the . . . the sign of the cross, like?

Pause.

SHARP: Er . . . yeah. (*Doing so.*) When we get down to that pub we'll toast him. Only a few pints worth because we've got some bulling to do tonight and everything's got to be right. Anyway, he wouldn't want us sitting round po-faced and piss miserable. We'll have a drink on his behalf . . . most sensible thing to do I reckon . . . I think so anyway . . . so would he, I reckon. (*They go.*)

GOLDY: Life has to go on right? Welcome home Terry.

In a carpark of pub. Piggy backs or perched on shoulder. POLO on DENIS, WALTERS on SHARP. GOLDY comes on first, holding a can of lager.

DENIS (*shouting to someone, off*): Goodnight.

WALTERS: You were lucky to have us. Lucky to have us grace your pokey little bog of a pub. D'you know who we are?

SHARP: Course he knows. Everyone knows . . .

DENIS (*shouting off*): Don't take any notice . . . he's had too much to drink. What's your game, Walters?

WALTERS: Fuck off, I'm not drunk.

SHARP: We're going to challenge you.

DENIS: Challenge who?

SHARP: A contest. A duel. A clash. A bit of a joust, like those knights used to. In days of yore. To win honour for their kings and handkerchiefs from their ladies. Us versus you two.

WALTERS: A fight to the finish. Goldy can be referee. Make sure there's fair play according to the rules of the Geneva convention.

DENIS: All right.

POLO: When you say fight to the finish – what d'you mean exactly?

WALTERS: Till one of us falls to the floor. Waves the white flag. Surrenders.

POLO: Right – with ya.

SHARP: Get up that end then.

DENIS: Right.

WALTERS: One shot.

POLO: Two shots is pussy.

WALTERS: This is this.

POLO (*gun to head*): Bang.

WALTERS: Great the way they got the

blood spurting out of that dink's head. It looked like they'd really done it. De Niro was brilliant. Except for when he started crying. I didn't like that bit. It was embarrassing.

POLO: You're going to die, motherfucker, you're going to die. You're dead, motherfucker.

SHARP: Don't fart again Walters or I'll have to drop you.

WALTERS: Thought it might help us pick up a bit of speed. A bit of propulsion out the back motor.

POLO: Bubbles in the bath when you fart. Eat baked beans and you could make your own bubble bath.

GOLDY: Let us know when you're ready.

SHARP: Under starter's orders.

DENIS: Let's engage the wankers.

WALTERS: Go!

GOLDY *raises his arm, drops it. They fight – both pairs topple to the ground.*

WALTERS: Disqualify them fuckers – he was trying to squeeze me bollocks.

DENIS: He was trying to find something to grip onto, but you've only got two fingers worth.

POLO: I feel sick.

WALTERS: We'll have to have a re-match.

DENIS: Some other time.

POLO: I'm going to be sick, I can feel it.

WALTERS: You know, if you got on the scales with a hard on, would you weigh more than normal?

DENIS: Don't start getting philosophical.

SHARP: Here Polo, guess what we're having for supper. We're having pilchards and custard, runny egg, sausages oozing with grease and a cup of tea with green bits floating in it. Foreign bodies. Oh – and fried bread smeared with axle grease.

POLO: Thanks a lot. I feel so much better since you told me that.

POLO *gets up, staggers over to the side to be sick.*

WALTERS: I don't think Polo'll be wanting any supper corp.

SHARP: You're quiet, Goldy. What's the matter?

GOLDY: Nothing. I'm just waiting for the sing-song to start. So I can join in, like.

WALTERS: I can't move.

DENIS: What?

WALTERS: I can't fucking move. Jesus Christ, I can't get up. I can't feel me legs!

SHARP: Stop fucking about.

WALTERS: Help me, help me! It's me back corp, me spine!

SHARP: Diddums hurtums?

WALTERS: When I fell – please corp, I'm not joking. I can't feel nothing. Numb, I feel numb.

SHARP: Help him up.

GOLDY: No, don't touch him – it might be dangerous if you move him. (*Pause.*) Can you feel your fingers? Does it hurt when I do this?

WALTERS: I can't feel fuck all! What are you doing – pinching me, punching me – tell us for fuck's sake! I'm scared – oh fuck – I don't like.

POLO: He won't be able to do the ceremonial tomorrow.

SHARP: Shut up you prick. You'll be all right Wally – we'll get an ambulance. (*To* POLO.) Go and find a telephone box! Now!

WALTERS: I'm cold. I'm shivering. Oh shit.

POLO: I saw a bloke fall off a ladder once. He looked like that.

GOLDY: Give us your jackets.

SHARP: Put this one under his head.

POLO: Maybe he's slipped his disc.

SHARP (*to* POLO): Ambulance! Telephone! Move!

POLO *moves.*

DENIS: Any pain, can you feel any pain anywhere?

WALTERS: I don't know! I was just lying here, laughing – tried to get up. Couldn't move – can't. I can't be paralysed can I – I was only playing piggy backs for fuck's sake. Only having a laugh.

GOLDY: Don't worry – there's nothing to worry about.

SHARP: Did it hurt when you fell?

WALTERS: No . . . I was . . . all right. I feel so cold now.

DENIS: Why's he feel cold, Goldy?

GOLDY: I don't fucking know, do I?

WALTERS: I just wanna get up and I can't.

SHARP: You'll be all right Wally. Be an ambulance here in a minute. (*Pause.*) Duty officer and RSM'll go fucking spare if they find out how it happened. Can't make something up — slipped on a fucking bar of soap or something. Bollocks – it's my fault, down to me. Shouldn't have been here in the first place. When they ask – I'll tell 'em – about the pratting about and drinking. I should have known better. Should have left that fucking pub an hour ago. Down to me this is. I'm going to get fucking carpeted, put on a charge, they'll go fucking berserk. (*Pause.*) Where's that ambulance?

WALTERS (*pause*): Lads, eh lads.

GOLDY: What's the matter?

WALTERS: Are you . . . are you game for a laugh?

He starts laughing.

SHARP: No.

WALTERS: Had you going didn't I? Yes.

DENIS: Fucking idiot! Fucking thoughtless pratt.

SHARP: Polo! Polo! (*Shouting after him, going off stage for a moment.*)

GOLDY: We nearly called an ambulance for you, you stupid fucker.

WALTERS: Don't start on me – I've got a bad back.

SHARP (*coming back*): I hope you're game for a laugh.

WALTERS: I'm sorry corp, I was only having a game, a bit of a laugh.

DENIS: I'm holding me sides.

SHARP (*to the others*): Jump the fucker.

They attack him, start to take off his trousers and shirt.

You game for a laugh now, Walters?

WALTERS: I didn't meant it corp. Only joking . . . Pack it in, will ya.

POLO *returns.*

POLO: What's happening? I thought . . . I thought he couldn't move.

SHARP: He's made a miraculous recovery.

POLO: He's ticklish.

DENIS: Cunt was having us on.

POLO: Not even a twinge.

WALTERS: Oh leave it out, will ya. Don't fuck about. It's freezing. I'll catch pneumonia. Give us 'em back yeah. Please, come on, for fuck's sake.

POLO: Ambulance on its way.

They all stop dead in their tracks.

SHARP: You're joking.

POLO: I know.

SHARP: Everyone's a fucking comedian.

WALTERS: Give us me trousers back.

DENIS: Ian?

SHARP: No, you suffer for a bit. Do you good. (*Short pause.*) Right, now listen to this – all of you. I don't want no more games. Any more tricks, any more pissing about from any of you – and I'll do my fucking nut, I'll do my fucking pieces. All over you. All right. Remember that – fucking learn it off by heart. Remember why we're here. So be as good as gold, don't even fart unless you want a kicking. (*To* DENIS:) Give him his trousers back.

SHARP *goes to have a piss up against the wall.*

Do you know that you drink the same glass of water five times? The sewage system in this country is marvellous don't you think? Think about it.

POLO *thinks about it – runs off to be sick again.*

WALTERS: Do you really?

POLO: Don't say any more corp, do us a favour.

DENIS: Not about sewage anyway, eh Polo?

SHARP (*saying some of this while still pissing up against the wall*): D'you know what I think? I think we're wasted – all of us – and it's a tragedy, it's a crying shame. What have we had since we came back? Six weeks leave and drilling till we're blue in the face. We've done so much fucking drilling I'm surprised we haven't struck oil. But we've got so much more to give society, such a great contribution we could make to it. Get involved in the daily life of Britain. Muck in. Use our energies. And I get the feeling more and more, especially lately, I don't know about you, that people are wishing and waiting we'd do just that. The ordinary British man in the ordinary British street I'm talking about – who's seen what we can do, what we are. That is, when we're not drunk and spewing and pissing up against walls. They seem to reckon we possess a lot of the qualities that are sadly lacking in today's modern society – like control, organisation, self-respect, appreciation for authority, initiative, guts. Hard to believe a fucking word of that looking at you four. Some people think we should be doing something more useful, where we can use our skills, our expertise. And it's not as if this country is without its problems . . . and the police can't always cope can they? They've got their hands full looking out for traffic offences, giving directions to tourists. Poor buggers were out of their depth in Brixton, Bristol, Liverpool. There's a whole tidal wave of sewage building up and it's threatening to overcome and overrun this lovely little island of ours. There's a growing feeling that we can sort out the problems, deal with the difficulties, treat the sewage. Because we've proved ourselves. I like the idea of that. Cos I'm bored, to tell you the truth, aren't you? I'm quite looking forward to getting stuck into something again. I've got a taste for the real thing now and so have most of the other lads I've spoken to. Who knows, we might be digging coal soon – we already drive ambulances and fire engines when necessary. We could be the nation's nurse – looking after it when it's sick – or its nanny – giving it a smack when it's naughty. At least we're professional. I mean, don't you feel professional – now and again?

In the TAVR Centre. Gear/bags located variously. POLO is cleaning his boots.

GOLDY *is polishing the buttons on his uniform.* DENIS *has hung up his uniform and is brushing it down. Coffee, plastic cups, kettles.* WALTERS *is doing press-ups.*

WALTERS: I was signing autographs for 'em all after it, me. (*Pause.*) Fucking marines trying to claim the glory in Port Stanley eh? Trying to take our flag down – jealous cunts, bad losers. Typical though, weren't it? Just what you'd expect. But we got the flags up first, on the racecourse and in the town, two and a half hours before anyone else. If it hadn't been for us . . .

GOLDY: Two's up with that brush, Polo.

DENIS: This is so clean you could eat your dinner off it, as they say.

POLO: Wouldn't be for long if you did.

DENIS: Did what?

POLO: Eat your dinner off it. Especially if it was baked beans or something.

DENIS: Pillock.

WALTERS: You could put the story in a Victor comic annual and everyone'd think it was far fetched. (*Pause.*) Wicked about the spic who lost his head though wasn't it?

DENIS: What you talking about?

WALTERS: You know . . . some of the lads took a photo of it and sent the photo to the bloke's wife in Buenos Aires. Just an head in a helmet!

DENIS: Oh yeah – they found a letter from her on his body. Her address was on it.

WALTERS: Body was up the other end of the trench. Talk about RSVP eh? She was probably expecting a letter to come back signed 'Yours forever, Carlos', And I always thought being out of your head meant you was stoned. Talk about RSVP eh? That's a good 'un. I shouldn't be sweating.

GOLDY: It means you're getting all the impurities out of your system with the help of your active glands. It's the body's own ventilation system. That's scientifical that is, that's a medical fact. (*Pause.*) D'you know you can get Falkland Islands purses, bags and brooches and Task Force T-shirts, posters and tea towels. Then there's the video and the board game and someone's made a record. It's called *The Falklands Spirit.*

WALTERS: That slow march has got to be as tight as a virgin's cunt tomorrow.

DENIS: You've got a lovely way with words, Wally.

WALTERS: Our balls'll be on parade. If we don't get anything but praise and approval our arses won't touch the ground. They'll be permanently lost in space along with our teeth.

DENIS: I've done two since I've been in. Two friends. This is the third friend. The first time, I was told soldiers can't bury another soldier and do justice to him with tears streaming down their faces, snot sniffing in their noses and sobs coming out of their throats. The second time I must have been getting the hang of it because I had time to notice that the bloke bearing in front of me had dandruff. And now it's being compared to a virgin's cunt. Talk about the march of progress. It's a funny old business innit?

DENIS *gets down to do some press-ups.*

Get rid of all the shit and filth and excess. Get some pain in me face.

GOLDY: Chase out all the impurities.

DENIS: And all impure thoughts, eh?

WALTERS: Goldy suffers from that don't you Goldy? Impure thoughts. Better get on the deck with Denis – get it out of your system. Cleanse yourself of all impurities.

GOLDY: Unlike you, of course.

WALTERS: I'm pure. Pure soldier me. One hundred per cent.

DENIS: No one is a hundred per cent. No one's pure. We all hesitate, we all know what it's like to shit it, to panic. As soon as you start to think you're perfect, that you can't go wrong, that's when you're fucked. Shouldn't ever forget that you can't hack it on your own, that's not the way it works. You need your oppo, you need the back up of your platoon, your company. Working together you might be a hundred per cent, as part of a unit you might be pure. On your own you're fuck all – it's comic book stuff to kid yourself otherwise. John Wayne crap.

WALTERS: Some people are more pure

than others, Denis. I'm one of those. One of the stronger links in the old chain.

The lights are suddenly switched off.

DENIS: What the fuck? The lights have gone.

SHARP (*in the darkness*): This photographer's taking pictures of a model for Penthouse. She's lying on this bed, legs up in the air, pussy out on display and he wants a close up but when he gets there – the smell nearly knocks him over. Talk about anchovies. So he tries to use a long lens but the pen and ink's still too much. So he tells her. You smell his says, down there. It's putting me off taking the pictures. What d'you mean she says, I keep it clean, I bathe it daily. Bathe it daily he says, who's he?

The lights are switched on again.

DENIS: Fucking hell.

WALTERS: That's a fucking good one. (*Laughing.*) Bathe it daily – who's he?

POLO: Oh I get it. Not David Bailey. Bathe it daily. Oh yeah.

SHARP: That was Fisher on the 'phone. He'll be meeting us at the house in the morning. How we getting on then?

DENIS: Lovely.

SHARP (*to* POLO): Give us that coffee up.

POLO: Pity I couldn't get no milk to go with it.

SHARP: Tragic innit? And there was me expecting a club biscuit as well.

POLO: There's this powder stuff. Coffeemate or something. You can get it when you run out of milk. Unless you take it black that is. Anyway, it's supposed to make the coffee taste better. You know they did a survey in the *Daily Mirror* . . .

WALTERS: Shut up you. Tomorrow we're going to a ceremonial and you want to talk about milk.

POLO: Coffee . . . I was talking about coffee, wanker.

GOLDY: Is it all right if I go out and get a bit of fresh air, Ian?

SHARP: What about them? (*Indicating his boots.*)

GOLDY: I'll finish 'em when I come back.

SHARP: Don't be long or I'll smack your bottom.

DENIS: I'm going to join him, Ian, all right?

SHARP: What's this – a fucking party game? Is the last one left the bloke with the personal hygiene problem or what? Or d'you just wanna hold each other's hands and willys under the moonlight?

DENIS: I'm already spoken for.

SHARP: Ten minutes.

WALTERS (to GOLDY): Do your fucking press-ups first.

SHARP: Ain't you done 'em yet?

GOLDY: Didn't know you took a personal interest in my welfare, Wally.

WALTERS: We've all been on the deck and you ain't done fuck all.

SHARP: You could do 'em when you come back, Goldy.

WALTERS: And we can all watch.

GOLDY (facing WALTERS): You like watching me do ya?

WALTERS: Want to make sure you do 'em properly.

GOLDY: So you'll know better in future, eh?

WALTERS: I know better now.

SHARP: Watch it you two.

GOLDY: No problem is there Wally?

WALTERS: No problem at all.

GOLDY: Something I been wanting to tell you for ages Wally.

WALTERS: Oh yeah.

GOLDY: Been wanting to get off my chest.

WALTERS: That right?

GOLDY gently rests his hands on WALTERS and even more gently kisses him on the cheek.

GOLDY: I love you Wally.

WALTERS (moving away): Fuck off! Fucking queer, bum bandit! What d'you think you're doing – kissing me, saying you love me, what's your fucking game?

GOLDY: Nothing wrong with love, is there? I can't help me feelings. And that's the way I feel. I love you, Wally. I wanna kiss you, I wanna give you a big hug.

WALTERS: Piss off! Fucking headcase you.

GOLDY: Still worried about me press-ups Wally?

WALLY doesn't respond: has backed away.

SHARP: D'you love me Goldy?

GOLDY: Course.

SHARP: Do you?

GOLDY: You know I do. Don't you believe me? If I could prove it, I would.

SHARP: Why don't you kiss me?

GOLDY: Later – when we're alone. I'll give you a French kiss.

SHARP: Your tongue in my mouth, eh Goldy?

GOLDY: Whatever makes you feel good.

SHARP: And you.

GOLDY: I told you Ian – I love you.

SHARP: Ten minutes.

GOLDY and DENIS outside, having a smoke.

DENIS: I was reading the other day that if the population of China jumped up and down at the same time there'd be tidal waves, earthquakes, and half of south-east Asia would subside into the ground. Let's hope the fuckers never get into punk, eh?

GOLDY: There's a new shop opened where me mum and dad live – it's called a Chinese bring it back.

DENIS: I had an Indian throw away the other night. I know someone who sent back his chicken tikka because it weren't chicken. And when the manager came over and said it was off the bone breast, this bloke said well I've never seen a chicken with a fucking tail, have you? (Pause.) D'you think the telly or papers'll cover it?

GOLDY: Dunno. Locally maybe. No one

wants a lot of fuss, do they? Anyway, I think it was easier welcoming home the *Hermes*. More human interest like. Interviewer asking 'And what are your plans for when you get back home tonight, ha ha' – 'Well, I'm going to have twenty-three pints of lager down at the local and then I'm going to have a bit of you know what with me girlfriend ha ha.'

DENIS: Might be a similar sort of feeling tomorrow.

GOLDY: No. He can't be interviewed tomorrow can he, saying how great it is to be home. He won't be making no V-signs or thumbs up. No one'll be waving unions jacks.

DENIS: There'll be one on the coffin though.

GOLDY: Yeah. (*Pause.*) You bulled up?

DENIS: More or less.

GOLDY: How's Linda?

DENIS: She's all right. The little 'un has just started walking.

GOLDY: You'll have to watch him like an hawk now I would have thought.

DENIS: I bought one of those gate things – stop him wandering out. Linda's hoping he won't work out how to push the latch thing up. (*Pause.*) He's only just getting used to me again.

GOLDY: What d'you mean?

DENIS: Well, when I came back, when we came back, he didn't know me, he'd forgotten who I was. Every time I went near him he started crying. Upset me a bit, but like, three months is a long time for a little kid. It's all right now – he lets me pick him up. When he laughs he pokes his tongue out at the same time.

GOLDY: I bet if you had a photo on ya you'd be showing me, eh?

DENIS: Course I would.

GOLDY: Who's a sentimental little pad then?

DENIS: I fucking am.

GOLDY: Daddy.

DENIS: He's luckier than some. Not just the dads that got killed either. It's the ones that come back like Sandy did – without his fucking legs. Just a pad like me – with a daughter. I mean, there might be a pension for him but what's he going to do now . . . work in a toy factory that'll employ him to sew noses on teddy bears? When he came back they promised him he could stay in.

GOLDY: He's still at Chessington . . .

DENIS: Being rehabilitated . . . I know. (Pause.) What makes me laugh is that I didn't even catch a fucking cold in those three months.

Pause.

GOLDY: Have you ever realised that if you're us you can't ever say hold on, just a minute, I don't know if I believe that, are you sure? You can't ever . . . disagree . . .

DENIS: About what?

GOLDY: Well, anything . . . everything . . . if you're us.

DENIS: You're not paid to have a conscience, you're paid to do what you're trained for. And you do as you're told, you respond – very fucking quickly, otherwise . . .

GOLDY (*interrupting*): I know. (*Pause.*) We might not be burying Terry.

DENIS: What?

GOLDY: Tomorrow – we might not be burying him. I know I shouldn't be thinking it, I don't know where the thought came from – but we might be burying turkey giblets tomorrow or two dead sheep or a few buckets of sand. How would we know, eh?

DENIS: No way Goldy, there's no way . . . everything . . . everything . . . that couldn't happen – they wouldn't do that. They brought up the bodies . . . straight to the ship . . . oh fuck . . . that's horrible.

GOLDY: I know I carried the body bag, I know his death was a tidy one but all of a sudden it don't seem hard to believe that me best friend's not really in that coffin at all. Turkey giblets or a boxful of dirt or someone else even. It's maybe a bit sick, I know, but it's hard to be certain about a lot of things now.

DENIS: Well, if there was a better way to have sorted it all out, it's too late now. The politics and that – it's nothing to do with us. And it wasn't at the time either.

GOLDY: When I found out they'd brought 2,000 body bags, I went and spewed up over the side of the ship. (*Pause.*) Who's this coming out? Quick – over here!

DENIS: What for – what you doing?

GOLDY: Come on!

They hide.
POLO comes out.

POLO: Goldy? Denis? You out here? Eh? (*Pause.*) He's sent me out for you. (*He hears a noise, turns quickly.*) What the fuck? Denis! Is that you? Don't fuck about. (*Pause.*) Come out, come out wherever you are. (*Pause.*) Come on, I don't want to hang about here all night. Stop pissing about will ya. Here Goldy, did I tell you I might be going to see UB40 in a couple of weeks time – they're playing in Reading. I can get you a ticket. He don't sound white does he – the singer?

GOLDY *cries out* POLO's *name as if distressed, followed by a loud frightening scream.*

Goldy – you all right? Goldy – where are you? Answer me! Answer me you bastard! Denis! 'If you see me walking down the street and I start to cry each time we meet, walk on by' – Dionne Warwick. It was written for her specially. Strangler did a cover version in 1980 – so did Average White Band.

A bottle smashes, another yell and GOLDY *groaning for help.*

'You're going to die, motherfucker! You're dead!' De Niro when they're slapping him in the hut. 'Show 'em your balls, Stevie, show 'em your balls. Put the gun to your head, pull the trigger. You can do it, you can do it.' I'll show you my balls wankers. I'm looking for you, I'll find you and give you a slap. (*Pause.*) It's fucking freezing out here – what d'you wanna play hide-and-seek for? There's nothing wrong is there?

DENIS *calls out 'Look out Polo'* – POLO *turns swiftly and as he does so,* GOLDY *comes from behind and puts his hands over his eyes.*
DENIS *pulls* POLO's *legs away.* POLO *falls down shouting.*

Fuck off you bastards!

GOLDY: Did you want us Polo?

POLO: 'Giant steps are what you take, walking on the moon – I hope your legs don't break, walking on the moon.'

In bed. The middle of the night.

POLO: Goldy?

GOLDY: What's the matter?

POLO: Did I tell you that Depêche Mode might be splitting up?

GOLDY: No, but I'm sure I'll get over it.

POLO: Be a shame if they did – I really liked their first LP — what's your favourite single of theirs? *Leave in Silence* is mine.

GOLDY: Go to sleep, Polo.

POLO: They come from Basildon. Did you know?

GOLDY: We've got to be up at six.

POLO: Funny name innit – Depêche Mode. It's French.

GOLDY: For fuck's sake – shut up and let me kip.

POLO: I just thought – you might want to talk.

GOLDY: I want to sleep. Don't you?

POLO: I don't want to dream.

GOLDY: Why?

POLO: Reminders . . . y'know . . . coming in me head. Kilby's hair flying about in the wind and the hole in his neck. I saw him . . . he was dead but his hair was moving . . . fell just below this ridge . . . and still nowhere near Boca Hill. Didn't know what to do . . . too scared to cry, wished I'd been in one of the other companies. Someone was shouting at me to get his belt . . . for the rounds it had left. I still hear the way he cried out and the noise of the mortars and the pucaras coming through the anchorage. Sometimes I hear 'em louder than other times – I brought 'em home with me – it's like they're stretching inside me head till there's no room left. Only thing worse is the quiet in between. The quiet was when we was waiting. When we had to wait – for the quiet to stop. I love records – they're normal. They're always on. Am I talking like a pratt Goldy?

GOLDY: No.

POLO: Kilby stopped hearing, stopped
being scared. Just his hair moving in the
wind. I dream about him . . . what a sniper
did. And when the doors of the school
house were opened – all the bodies . . .
like the charred wood on a burnt out
bonfire. All black and twisted together.
Not like real people. And now we've got
to bury Terry again. I was thinking,
before it started, that it'd be a bit like
going on exercise. (*Pause.*) I stuck a
bayonet in one of their bellies. It made a
sort of gurgling sound. I had it's blood on
me bayonet. I think I killed it. I just
behaved y'know. Stay awake with us
Goldy.

GOLDY: When you played soldiers when
you was a kid and someone shot you
dead, did you ever have to lie there
waiting for your mate to come and touch
you on the shoulder and say 'you're
released'? And then you was alive again,
it was all right to get up and carry on
making machine-gun noises . . .

POLO: And pull the pins out of hand
grenades with your teeth.

All right weren't it?

We're grown up now though. Big boys.

WALTERS: Will you two shut your fucking
traps and cuddle your teddy bears
instead. You might want to wake up
feeling like a garden slug but I don't. Big
day tomorrow – I wanna be ready for it.
Night night – sleep tight.

*Morning in the TAVR Centre. DENIS,
WALTERS, GOLDY and POLO are
putting on their uniforms with great
deliberation and care. SHARP enters,
fully dressed.*

SHARP: All right boys. Apparently it's
going to be a mild day today. Dry and
mild and just a slight breeze. A perfect
day in other circumstances. Polo, you
next. Best of three. (*They play knuckles.*)
Wiped away the remains of your wet
dreams have you, or d'you only have
sweet ones? I had a good night. We'll
make our way to the house about nine,
shall we? That'll give us plenty of time.

*SHARP proffers his two hands to
WALLY, both clenched.*

Come on Wally.

*WALTERS plays knuckles with SHARP.
SHARP wins two in a row. WALTERS is
rubbing his hands in pain afterwards.
SHARP beats DENIS similarly and
likewise hurts him. Every time a game is
won the winner slaps the loser in the face.*

Goldy. Your turn.

GOLDY: I haven't finished.

SHARP: Fucking get up! You can finish
bulling when you've joined in with this.
You do want to join in don't you?

*They play. GOLDY wins the first,
SHARP the second.*

One all then. Last one. Close innit?
Exciting. You've done well to get this far.

SHARP wins the last one.

GOLDY: You win, corp.

SHARP: That was for your benefit not
mine. I bet you feel better already. Wakes
you up doesn't it?

GOLDY: Not half.

SHARP: Great. (*Pause. To all of them.*)
Don't go away.

SHARP goes.

WALTERS: What were you two
whispering about last night?

GOLDY: You.

DENIS: We'd better give ourselves plenty
of time to get to the house. Is Fisher going
to meet us there?

GOLDY nods.

POLO: Me stomach feels funny.

SHARP re-enters with Union Jack Flag.

SHARP: No creases, no marks right?
Right?

The flag is re-folded.

DENIS: Is the church far from the house?

GOLDY: About a quarter of a mile.

SHARP: Been to services more times in the
last few months than a priest.

WALTERS: You must know the roll of
honour off by heart, Ian.

SHARP: I should. We all should. Every
name on it is a reminder of just how much
this country is prepared to stand up for
what it believes in and defend its

territory. In our case, forty-four blokes who gave the paras an even better reputation than it had before, who lost their lives making fucking greasy tinpot dictators see that no piece of Britain is there for the taking. Civilians will never have that opportunity, that challenge – a lot of 'em wouldn't be prepared, wouldn't be able to face up to it. That makes every one of the forty-four bloody special and rare. You remember that when we're carrying Terry today.

GOLDY *grabs the Union Jack, backs away with it, holds a lighter to it.*

What the fuck . . . ?

GOLDY: Sick of hearing about Terry dying for his country, prepared to pay the price for . . . for what eh?

SHARP: Give us that back.

DENIS: For fuck's sake Goldy, don't be stupid . . .

WALTERS: Are you fucking mental? He's gone fucking mental.

POLO: Stop it Goldy, you'll get yourself into trouble.

GOLDY: This ain't so fucking important . . . so fucking holy. (*He laughs.*) Tradition. What's it going to do . . . Sanctify everything . . . make it honourable . . .

DENIS: What do you think you're doing?

SHARP: You do anything to that . . . and you'll be fucking us up, you won't be doing many favours to yourself either, you stupid cunt. Worst of all, you'll be insulting him and his family.

GOLDY: We used to go fishing – me and him. He caught a pike once – scared the fuck out of him. I nearly pissed meself laughing. We used salt and vinegar crisps as bait once. It worked. No more fishing now.

SHARP (*very reasonable*): You're doing this for yourself, not him. Terry wouldn't appreciate, wouldn't be thanking you. I don't know what the fuck you think you're doing anyway – I know you've been under a lot of pressure, we all have, but you're making a pratt of yourself. It's going to be hard enough for his family today as it is – and they wanted him buried this way – you have to realise that. Today

should be remembered as the day we buried a bloody good soldier, someone we can all be proud of and do justice to. It shouldn't have to be remembered as the day his best friend let him down and embarrassed his family and his mates. Come on. Please. You don't mean it. And you don't deserve the trouble you'd get in, the shit you'd have to take.

Pause.

GOLDY *hands it back to* SHARP *who in turn places it on one of the beds. Having done so he pulls* GOLDY *down, kicks him three times in the ribs.*

Pause.

SHARP *begins to help* GOLDY *up.*

Come on fellah, up you get, it's not serious. I'm sorry about that, well sort of – but you're a silly boy you know. What the fuck was all that about anyway? No need for that. You were the one kicking dead bodies in the bollocks and in the head when you found out about Terry. You hated, you was warry. What's all this protest shit? You've forgotten the most important thing – you do what you're told and you don't do anything else. The most important way you learn that is physically. Like just then. I'm not going to say a word about this – not to Price or anyone else. All right?

GOLDY: Cheers. Thanks corporal. Ian.

GOLDY *continues to get ready for the ceremonial.*

TERRY's *front room.* DENIS, GOLDY, POLO, SHARP, WALTERS *and* FISHER *are standing around the coffin. The coffin is draped in the Union Jack.*

SHARP: He's been brought home 8,000 miles and his journey's not over yet. This is the most important part of that journey. Let's give him the best welcome home we can. The last welcome home. (*Pause.*) OK lads? (*He places Terry's beret on the coffin.*)

GOLDY: Yes Ian, yeah.

SHARP: Polo?

POLO: All right.

SHARP: Bearer party – lift!

The coffin is lifted onto their shoulders.
They slow march to music.

POLO *back in the TAVR Centre. he goes*
to cassette tape recorder which he has either
hidden or locked away somewhere. He turns
it on. He is fraught, very upset. He takes it
into a corner, sits huddled with it. He turns
the music off as SHARP *enters.*

SHARP: You cunt.

POLO: Sorry.

SHARP: You made us look like pratts.

POLO: Got to me a bit – sorry about that.

SHARP: Fucking sorry! What the fucking
hell use is sorry – there's no such thing as
sorry for us you wanker – there ain't
supposed to be no need for it – sorry's a
fucking mistake, something, someone
gone wrong, a fuck up – apologies in this
game are a fucking joke, they're obscene.
You don't offer your sorries when you
can't do your job – you get fucking done,
you get punished. You don't get
understood, you don't get forgiven – you
get shat on – s'how you learn why you
have to do it right – all the fucking time.

POLO: The occasion, like . . . me nerves . . .
upset, like.

SHARP: You didn't have to say sorry at
Boca or Wireless Ridge. None of us had
to say sorry nowhere on that fucking
island – s'what makes us professional,
s'why we pulled it off. Don't talk to me
about the occasion.

POLO (*screaming out*): I didn't like it!

SHARP: You was out of step twice! You
was supposed to be a bearer – not a
fucking liability. We nearly had to stop!

POLO: I know . . . I know (*Pause.*) I'm a
toe-rag, it's down to me. I know. Cunt . . .
me. I've let you all down. (*Pause.*) You
going to give me a kicking?

SHARP: Gotta go and see Price tomorrow.
Fuck knows what he's going to do. Mr
and Mrs General Public thought it was all
very proper . . . they always do. But that's
not good enough. (*Furious again.*) Ten
ton of shit is going to get dropped on me
tomorrow!

POLO: Hurt me. You can if you want.

Trouble I've made. Kick me fucking head
in . . . knock some sense into me . . . What
am I, eh? I'm supposed to be a para . . .
the best . . . not an arsehole, eh? Not an
arsehole . . . a bottle job . . . a wally. I
need to be put into line . . . hurt.
Punished.

SHARP: I ought to take you apart.

POLO: Do it! (*Pause – and then as if he's*
just had an idea.) Look I'll help you . . .
something else . . . this . . . look. (*Turning*
on music again.) Discipline . . . I'll help
you out, like a good unit . . . a good
company . . . working for each other.

SHARP: What the fucking hell are you
going on about?

POLO: The colonel said . . . about the
whole operation . . . over there . . . a good
team effort . . . working together . . . a
team. I'll dance.

Getting up.

SHARP: You're cracked, you stupid
bastard.

POLO: Grin made me do it that time . . . not
on guard duty. Caught me. A fitting
punishment. His sense of humour.
Humiliate. Humiliate me. Made me feel
like a pratt. (*He is dancing by now.*) Look
. . . look . . . Ian . . . corporal . . .
punishment . . . I deserve it . . . put me on
a charge as well, make me do a dance.
Look stupid, ridiculous. Teach me a
lesson.

The others come in, unnoticed by SHARP
and POLO.

Make me look like the pratt I am! I'm
supposed to be a soldier . . . I'm nothing
. . . I'm supposed to be a cherry beret . . .
I'm fucking useless. I'm dancing . . .
you're making me dance . . . for bringing
the regiment into disrepute.

SHARP *shaking head, half in resignation,*
half in disbelief.

DENIS: What's going on? Silly bastard –
look at him.

WALTERS: Thinks he's being funny.

DENIS: Is he taking the piss Ian or what?

WALTERS: Nothing to fucking laugh
about.

DENIS: You're a scream, Polo – a right

joker. You auditioning for *Top of the Pops*?

WALTERS: John Travolta, ain't he?

DENIS: You got Saturday night fever Polo?

WALTERS: This ain't a fucking disco. There's no flashing lights.

SHARP: He's not joking.

WALTERS: Eh?

SHARP: I said he's not joking! He fucking means it – it ain't a joke.

WALTERS: You mean . . .

SHARP: You can see what I mean.

DENIS: Fucking hell.

WALTERS: A wobbly.

SHARP (*to* POLO): Fucking stop it! Pack it up!

Pushing him away and taking the cassette. He stops it.

WALTERS: State of him.

DENIS: Polo – sit down will ya. You'll be all right. Sit still. Give it a rest eh?

SHARP: Done enough fucking damage for one day.

WALTERS: Yeah.

DENIS: Weren't that serious.

SHARP (*turning on* DENIS): Doesn't matter – it wasn't right – he fucked it!

POLO: Can I have me music back please?

SHARP: Anyone'd think he was a fucking child.

POLO: Can I have me music back please?

WALTERS: It's been confiscated.

POLO: Please – me music.

SHARP: Look at him, look. He's supposed to be one of us.

DENIS: He is.

SHARP: He was.

DENIS (*to* POLO): Relax, kid, there's nothing to worry about. (*To the others.*) He needs a break – he'll be all right. S'all he needs . . . a bit of a rest. (*To* POLO *again:*) D'y'wanna fag Polo, sit down with us and have a flash, yeah? Come on, stop being silly.

POLO: Me music, me cassette. Give it back – bit off today, not on me old form. Different tomorrow. I'll be better tomorrow. Me old self. Give us.

WALTERS: Look at the way he's going on! He's lost control I'm telling ya!

SHARP: I could kill you, you pathetic bastard. (*He throws the cassette to* WALTERS.) Not content with fucking up the ceremonial . . .

DENIS: We buried a mate for fuck's sake. An hour ago we buried a mate!

SHARP: You don't have to tell me – but we were asked to be bearers for him – in full view. (*Pause.*) I've got an appointment with Price and the adjutant tomorrow, you know that don't ya – wait till they find out about this fucking finale.

POLO: Don't break it. Please. Wally, come on Wally. I'll show you how to change the bass and treble, I'll show you how to louden it up. I'll show you how it works. I'll show you. You'll break it. Be careful. Be careful.

DENIS: Give it back to him.

SHARP: No! Not yet Wally, not yet. Hang on to it.

DENIS: You'll make it worse, don't wind it up.

POLO: Yeah, give us it back – you'll make it worse.

SHARP: You don't deserve it. You're . . . you're in disgrace. Ain't that right Wally – eh?

WALTERS (*not sure what's going on*): Er . . . yeah. In disgrace yeah.

SHARP: You've been a naughty boy, hasn't he Wally?

WALTERS: Yeah.

SHARP: Your bottom needs a good spanking.

WALTERS (*catching on*): No sweets for you.

SHARP: Straight to bed without any tea and no light left on on the landing.

DENIS: Don't treat him like that! Polo – leave it. They're only pissing about – let 'em get on with it.

WALTERS: Daddy'll be home soon.

SHARP: Give you a good telling off. Only good boys can play with their cassette.

DENIS: For fuck's sake.

SHARP: Have you said your prayers, have you brushed your teeth?

WALTERS: Shall mummy kiss you goodnight?

POLO: Bastards. Bastards. Stop being horrible, stop being nasty. Fuck off. I fought the Argies.

During the preceding sequence, POLO's 'music', his tape cassette, will be passed between WALTERS and SHARP, alternately going behind each other's back to receive it. When SHARP is receiving it, WALTERS will have the cassette hiding behind his back with both hands, and vice versa. When SHARP has taken it and put it behind his back WALTERS will show open palms to POLO as if to say 'look' – it must be done briskly, cleverly.
DENIS will try and come between these two. POLO and GOLDY will do nothing except watch. Suddenly POLO picks something up – a weapon – he threatens them with it.

I fought the Argies! Don't try and make a fool of me you cunts, don't take me for no clown – I'm a hard bastard, hard as nails. I'm a cherry beret, a fucking killer. I've killed! I'll do ya! I'll take you out!

SHARP: You're a non-starter.

WALTERS: A wank.

SHARP: You're not capable – you haven't got it. You couldn't bruise an apple anymore. You've gone wonky – look at ya.

DENIS: This is fucking crazy! We gotta break it up, Goldy!

POLO: I'm trained and experienced, I'm fit! I'm a fitness fanatic! Strong as a fucking lion I am. So don't get clever – I know what I'm doing, I've got training, I've got skills and two service medals! I'll hammer the pair of you – no trouble – not for someone like me. I'm a professional soldier.

SHARP: Come on then – let's see you have a fight. Let's see you do something.

POLO: I will. I will in a minute.

SHARP: What's wrong with now! Come for me, hate me, fight me! I wanna see your

instinct, I wanna see your pedigree! I wanna see you hack it!

POLO: No trouble.

DENIS: Put that down Polo – forget it, there's no need. Don't let 'em wind you up, don't let 'em bait you. Throw it down, now! Goldy!

GOLDY: Nothing to do with me.

SHARP: Have you still got it, have you got it left? Show me you're a soldier, come on! Show me what you're supposed to be. All you've got to show are the fucking clothes – you got no right to be wearing 'em. Are you the real thing or a fucking imposter, are you twenty-four carat or not? I heard you was an hero. That can't be right. Hurt me, hate me! Steam in, put the boot in, nut me! Where's your bottle?

WALTERS (to POLO): Go on! Prove yourself! Hack it! Hack it! Hack it!

SHARP: You're not going to shit out are you? I've seen you in action taking out a trench. I've seen you throwing phosphorus, pushing forward. You weren't scared then, you weren't bricking it then.

DENIS: Fucking leave him alone!

SHARP: He's threatening us – trying to. Let him. It's better than what he was doing before. A dance! At least this is fucking normal! He hasn't done the most important thing though yet – have you son? He's all mouth. He's all bark and no bite! He's a pretender.

DENIS (to GOLDY): What's a matter with you – standing there like a fucking spare prick – you was the disgusted one, now sort this out with us – I need your fucking help. Someone's going to get hurt for nothing in a minute.

GOLDY: I'm not involved.

DENIS: You're fucking wrong!

SHARP (about GOLDY): He's staying where he is, he's using his discretion. Keeping a low profile – ain't that right Goldy? I can rely on him, he's as good as gold. Get it? He does as he's told. He's come up trumps. He's a good 'un, he's keeping his mouth shut – aren't you fellah?

GOLDY: Yeah.

DENIS: Thanks. Ta. Cheers. Friend.

Mucker. I thought you . . . cared.

WALTERS (*to* POLO): Mouth and trousers, let's see what you got.

SHARP: Not a lot.

WALTERS: I'll take care of you anytime.

SHARP: He's challenging you.

WALTERS: Offering you out.

DENIS (*to* GOLDY): Feel something for fuck's sake!

GOLDY: I do.

DENIS: Show us then!

SHARP (*to* POLO): Are you up to it?

WALTERS: Can you face it?

SHARP: A row.

WALTERS: A staightener.

SHARP: Are you a brown trouser job?

WALTERS: Yellow. Cowardy custard.

SHARP: Come on!

POLO: I'm dangerous, I'm special. (*Pause.*) Grin used to say . . . Grin said . . . a joke . . . a sort of joke – you will be faster than a speeding train . . .

At this point GOLDY *begins to walk over to* POLO.

SHARP: What the fuck you doing! Piss off!

POLO: You will leap buildings at a single bound . . .

SHARP (*to* GOLDY): I'm warning you toe-rag – keep out of this – let him do it, he wants to do it.

DENIS *picks something up to keep* SHARP *and* WALTERS *from interfering with* GOLDY.

What's your game? I'll have your bollocks for breakfast Denis, I'm telling ya!

DENIS: Putting a stop to all this. You all right Goldy?

GOLDY: Lovely.

SHARP: Don't interfere – he needs to stand up for himself, he mustn't let anyone shit on him. He's got to fight back. Let him get a bit of self-respect back, a bit of pride. S'what makes him, s'what makes all of us. He needs to hate again, fight. It'll help him – can't you see that, can't you understand?

GOLDY: Feel like a man eh?

SHARP: He's supposed to be a professional soldier in the best fucking battalion in the best fucking regiment there is. Let him feel like it. (*Pause.*) I didn't get this (*Indicating stripe.*) by quivering in a corner and letting people get the better of me. I didn't get this by being unsure and ashamed – I believed in myself, I set standards for myself, and I pulled myself up and made people notice what I had going for me. I liked myself. Does he right now? Let him start throwing punches, give him the chance to stop feeling like a used durex, like . . . nothing.

GOLDY *has put his hand on* POLO's *free arm, holding out his other hand for* POLO *to give him the weapon.*

POLO: You will have X-ray vision, bullets will bounce off your bodies. You will not, I am sorry to say, get to wear a cloak and you will only fly downwards but I can promise you this – you will have no fear of Kryptonite.

GOLDY *slowly takes the weapon from* POLO.

I fought the Argies.

GOLDY *throws the weapon down, holds* POLO.

GOLDY: It's all right mate, you're all right.

SHARP (*to* DENIS *and* GOLDY): Happy now the pair of you?

GOLDY (*to* POLO): Your face is getting wet you sloppy bugger. Wipe it on your sleeve.

WALTERS: Is he crying?

GOLDY: Yeah – he's crying. And not only that – he's trembling, like a little dog who's been left out in the cold and there's snot on his fuckin' chin. And I'm hugging him cos . . . cos . . I want to . . . cos he might need it. I know I do sometimes. Are you watching me, can you see me? (*Pause.*) He won't be steaming in today, won't be sticking his chest out and trying to sort you out – not today. Your psychology's a bowl of piss – he don't get his dignity from being ready to put the boot in and have a war with anyone who upsets him. No one does.

SHARP: You prefer him like that, do ya?

GOLDY: Better than the way Terry ended up innit?

WALTERS: He got respect anyway.

Pause.

GOLDY (*to* WALLY): I don't get you! Remember when you carried Terry down, Wally – it was you Wally – remember.

WALTERS: Course I fucking remember.

GOLDY: You brought him down from the hill Wally, you carried him. Why, Wally?

WALTERS: I couldn't fucking leave him there, could I? I couldn't leave him up there . . . dead.

GOLDY: You cared about him, didn't you Wally, you must have cared about him.

WALTERS: He was one of us. Someone had to.

GOLDY: But it was you.

WALTERS: Look, I don't want to talk about it. I just did it, all right. I don't want congratulations. I don't want appreciation. I couldn't leave him up there . . . he was one of us.

GOLDY: So is Polo, so is he. Him here. There's no difference – why are you pissing on him? He's not hacking it at the moment – so what? He's a mate, a mate. I wanna hold him, I want him to be all right, looked after. It's not embarrassing is it? I've got me arms round his shoulder and his head is on me chest. Don't you want to do the same – don't you? You can if you want. (*He laughs.*) I won't get jealous. Come on – it's nothing to be ashamed of. He's not well. That's all. He's not well. A bit of kindness . . . never hurt anyone. For fuck's sake. We can afford it, can't we? It don't stop us from being soldiers, does it?

WALTERS: He was all right when we came back – I was standing next to him. He was smiling and waving like the rest of us. And the past few months there's been nothing wrong. The MO would have noticed something, wouldn't he? He's always been a bit mad, a bit silly. That's Polo. But he was all right – wouldn't have been picked for the ceremonial otherwise.

SHARP: He shouldn't have gone like this . . . he's supposed to be one of us . . . he's supposed to be able to cope and do his job. I thought everything was going to be all right. (*Pause.*) I love this life, this world. Its certainty and strength, there's no confusion, there's no doubt and if there is, it gets stamped out, it gets dealt with. Eight years ago . . . joining up . . . me . . . it was like taking a blunt knife to a stone and since then I've achieved things, I fit in. I know what's expected of me and when – and I do it. And I know what to expect of other people. When you go onto civvy street . . . everything's so fucking complicated and mixed up – I'm not sure how I should behave – which ones do you call sir, eh? Me mum and dad have got a photo of me on their mantelpiece. They're proud. (*Pause.*) This . . . him . . . it's all a fucking mess . . . I couldn't have been doing me job properly. Mind you, somebody always gets upset at a funeral don't they? (*Pause.*) Has he stopped shaking yet?

RASPBERRY

Raspberry was first presented at the Edinburgh Festival on 30 August 1982, with the following cast:

CHRIS	Marion Bailey
EILEEN	Tilly Vosburgh
NURSE	Susanna Bishop

Directed by Adrian Shergold
Designed by David Roger

The production opened at the Soho Poly Theatre, London, on 14 September 1982.

Hospital – a four bed bay.
CHRISTINE *(thirty) is in bed.*
NURSE *(twenty) enters, followed by*
EILEEN *(seventeen).*

NURSE *(to* EILEEN): That's your bed there. Locker for your things is beside it.

EILEEN: Thanks. Ta. *(Taking off her coat.)*

NURSE: We're not finished yet.

Taking a thermometer from the wall.

I'm being trained for other things as well as showing people where their beds are. Like taking temperatures. It's all go.

She indicates for EILEEN *to sit down.*

Can you open your mouth please.

Watching her respiration, taking her pulse.

Blood pressure too, I'm afraid.

EILEEN *rolls up her sleeve,* NURSE *takes her blood pressure.*

That's lovely. Well done. We'll need to put our nightdress on after this, OK? I hope you remembered to bring it, did you?

EILEEN *tries to speak, with the thermometer still in her mouth.*

Try and keep it in, could you? Thanks.

Pause. She takes the thermometer out of EILEEN's *mouth.*

EILEEN: Shall I put it on in here?

NURSE: Either here or in the toilet, if you'd rather. Talking about toilets, I'll need a sample of your water. In this, as soon as you can, please. *(Indicating a tin container.)*

EILEEN: I've just been . . .

NURSE: Well, I'm sure you'll be able to manage it again in a bit. That's what bladders are for, according to the textbooks. *(Pause.)* Any valuables?

EILEEN: Sorry?

NURSE: Valuables. Have you got anything of value with you? Like an engagement ring or something. *(Pause.)* A gold cross or bracelet – anything like that. We'll need to take them away and look after them for you. Keep them safe.

EILEEN: Just this.

Taking a small gold chain from her neck.

NURSE: I'll get you a receipt. *(Pause.)* You'll be getting a wristband in a minute that you'll have to put on. For identification – it'll give your name, age, religion and hospital number. A plastic one. *(Pause.)* In case we forget who you are – and to make sure we're doing the right operation on the right person.

EILEEN: Where do I put my clothes?

NURSE *(pointing to the locker)*: Sorry – I thought I'd already told you. They'll probably get a bit creased in there however carefully you fold them but we can't have everything in life. Anyway, I should think that'll be the least of your problems tomorrow, when you . . .

EILEEN *(interrupting)*: I'm not bothered about me clothes getting creased . . .

Pause.

NURSE: You'll find the day-room at the bottom of the main ward should you want to smoke or watch *Crossroads* or whatever else takes your fancy. There's even daisy-patterned wallpaper in there to make it home from home. Feeding time is at five-thirty, visiting time six to eight. Payphone is by the lifts on the right, hospital shop is in the basement, radio and earphones are behind you, lights must be out by ten. *(Pause.)* Any make-up you're wearing or nail varnish on your toes or fingers will have to come off I'm afraid.

EILEEN: I'm on insulin.

NURSE: Oh yes that's right – it says so in the notes. *(Pause.)* All seems quite straightforward then. If there's anything you want to ask about don't be shy, will you. Do let us know. *(Pause.)* I'll just go and get some scales to weigh you, OK?

EILEEN: Weigh me?

NURSE: Yes – weigh you. Nothing out of the ordinary, we don't want your vital statistics or anything. It's for the anaesthetic – how much you'll need. It depends on weight. You do want an anaesthetic don't you?

EILEEN: Course I do. Not like a visit to the dentist's is it?

NURSE: That's right. Definitely no sweets at the end of it for being a good girl. *(Pause.)* This is Mrs Kaye by the way.

MRS KAYE: Chris.

EILEEN: Eileen – all right?

NURSE: Oh before I forget – I hope you brought some towels or tampons with you – there'll be quite a lot of bleeding afterwards. Heavier than your period. Unless you have exceptionally heavy periods.

EILEEN: I was told – by the doctor I saw.

NURSE: Good, right. He'll be round to see you later – to make sure it's still all systems go. (*Pause.*) Did you bring your green form?

EILEEN: Oh yeah. Here.

NURSE: Lovely. Thanks. (*Pause.*) HSA 1 – sounds innocuous enough doesn't it. At the bottom, anyway. I'll go and bring the scales then, OK? Screen's around the bed if you want to get dressed in here. All right then?

She goes.

CHRIS: If it's any consolation to you – she's not a qualified one. She's a student.

EILEEN: Perhaps when she's qualified she might like me.

CHRIS *and* EILEEN *coming back into the bay.*
EILEEN *is now wearing a nightdress.*

CHRIS: I think I'd rather chew a dirty bandage than eat those greens again. I should have brought some sandwiches of me own in. And a flask of tea. Could have had a picnic then couldn't I?

EILEEN: No grass.

CHRIS: Green blanket look.

EILEEN: You'll know better in future.

CHRIS: I'm hoping I don't have to come back. Not to this ward anyway.

EILEEN: Me as well.

Pause.

CHRIS: You been in hospital before, Eileen?

EILEEN: Only to have me tonsils out when I was a little girl.

CHRIS: They don't bother with tonsils now do they?

EILEEN: What d'you mean?

CHRIS: They don't take them out any more. Not unless you've got it bad.

EILEEN: I sounded like Minnie Mouse afterwards. Squeaky. Have you?

CHRIS: Have I what – sounded like Minnie Mouse?

EILEEN: No! Been in hospital before.

CHRIS: A few times, yeah. I don't think it's the sort of thing you can ever get used to though.

EILEEN: It's so warm in here. Giving me a headache.

CHRIS: I think the generators are directly beneath us.

EILEEN: Oh.

CHRIS: They always have the windows shut in hospitals as well, don't they? That don't help.

EILEEN *indicating the two other empty beds.*

EILEEN: I wonder if anyone else is coming in.

CHRIS: Could have a game of bridge then couldn't we?

EILEEN: I can't play cards.

CHRIS: That was a joke. (*Pause.*) Bloody itchy where they shaved me. Dying to scratch.

EILEEN: Will they do that to me? They didn't say anything.

CHRIS: I wouldn't think they need to in your case.

EILEEN: No.

CHRIS: Ask the nurse or doctor, rather, when he comes round.

EILEEN: Have you seen him yet – the doctor?

CHRIS: Not yet, no.

EILEEN: I hope he's all right – not funny or nasty or nothing.

CHRIS: Anyone comng to visit you, love?

EILEEN: Me mum might, I think. (*Pause.*) I've got a boyfriend as well. We've been going out a year, nearly.

CHRIS: Is he coming as well then?

EILEEN: He don't like hospitals. They make him nervous. He says you never know what you might see in a hospital. I think he expects to find the Elephant Man running up the corridor after him. He don't like the smell either. Smell of hospitals. Clean smells trying to cover up the bad ones he says.(*Pause.*) He bought me some chocolates though. Nice of him weren't it?

CHRIS: What's his name?

EILEEN: Steve. Apparently his mum had this big crush on Steve McQueen when she was pregnant. That's why she called him Steve, like.

CHRIS: Just as well she didn't like Yul Brynner then innit?

EILEEN *doesn't get it.*

EILEEN: I don't know why I just told you all that. I just didn't want you to think . . . you know . . . that I go with anyone. (*Pause.*) He's the only one . . . you know . . .

CHRIS: That you've slept with?

EILEEN (*quiet*): Yeah. (*Pause.*) I wouldn't want anyone to think I was a slag or anything. Especially like with you. I'd like you to know I was . . . (*Interrupted.*)

CHRIS: A decent girl?

EILEEN: Well . . . yeah.

CHRIS: Why – because I told you what I was in here for? (*Pause.*) Don't waste your time bothering about what I think. Anyway, decent girls ain't supposed to end up in here are they – that's what they say innit? They used to say decent girls didn't have sex, then they said decent girls don't get pregnant, and now decent girls definitely don't have abortions, because contraceptives are available and there's no excuse! So don't worry about all that decent bollocks, worry about something else. (*Pause.*) I've got some orange squash here – d'you want a drop?

Just after visiting time. EILEEN *and* CHRIS *are in bed.*

EILEEN (*quite agitated*): I suppose you guessed that was me mum just now.

CHRIS: I saw the likeness.

EILEEN: Did you see the tears?

CHRIS: Who were they for – her or you?

EILEEN: She . . . she . . . wanted me to have a white wedding see. She was hoping I would. More like set her heart on it. It's upset her a lot.

CHRIS: No one can stop you wearing white if you want to when you get married.

EILEEN: Yeah . . . but she thinks right . . . everyone'll know . . . . it won't be true . . . what it's supposed to mean.

CHRIS: What – about being 'pure'? I give up trying to be pure when I let a boy put his tongue in me mouth when I was thirteen. I was so ashamed I washed meself with Pears soap for a week afterwards to make meself feel pure again but it didn't make me feel any better. But I had to admit him putting his tongue in me mouth did, so I went back for some more.

EILEEN: French kissing's a bit different to . . . it's not the same thing – well for a start I'm not in here for French kissing am I?

Pause.

CHRIS: When I did me Holy Communion I was all in white. White sandals, white socks, white frock. I was Mum and Dad's little girl. I looked like a fucking ice-cream. White weddings are as much about being Mum and Dad's little girl as anything else.

EILEEN: It's supposed to be a special day. Can look like a princess.

CHRIS: Look pure. Like an ice-cream that no one's licked.

EILEEN: What about you – what did you do?

CHRIS: I got married in Poplar Civic Registry Office. Went in at eleven, came out at five past. It was funny really – my old nan came – had her best frock on – but she was so riddled with arthritis she could hardly move and by the time she managed to get her bum on the seat we was all on the way out again. Anyway, the confetti got thrown, the photos took and we all went round the hall. I had this navy skirt suit on with a pale blue silk blouse from Liberty's. Looked really nice. (*Pause.*) Can't say I felt as innocent and sweet as Doris Day or Isla St Clair but so what, eh?

EILEEN: I'm not . . . not really bothered . . . don't want all that fuss, don't even know if I want to get married. Or have kids. Don't know if I deserve to.

CHRIS: I want kids, s'why I'm lying here now – but it's nothing to do with deserving. I don't want 'em like a prize to be won or a reward that I've earned for being a fully grown woman. Mind you, sometimes I think I should get the VC for what I've put up with.

EILEEN: How d'you mean? Your treatment, like?

CHRIS: We'd been trying for a baby for two years before I went to me GP. Since then me legs have been up and down on so many different doctors couches they think they're a pair of windscreen wipers. Some of them think they're playing a game of snooker the way they poke things up you.

EILEEN: Your husband must have had tests as well though.

CHRIS: Oh yeah – he had to provide a specimen of his semen. But that's no hardship is it – all it meant was that he had to wank into a jar. No embarrassment, shame or discomfort for him. He just disappeared into the toilet with a sheepish grin on his face, one copy of Health and Efficiency and a bottle of cooking oil.

EILEEN: What – he used the cooking oil to . . .

CHRIS: Well, he couldn't really use a bottle of domestos could he. Yeah, all he had to do was make sure he got it all in the jar. But I was the one who had to take it up the hospital. It looked like a blob of salad cream.

EILEEN *breaks up.*

Well, it did. Especially in that jar. But you can see he was the one who was all right. Now it's given him the chance to feel protective instead of the opposite, which it would have been if . . .

EILEEN (*interrupting*): You must have been really upset when you found out.

CHRIS: So must you.

Pause.

EILEEN: It helps if people stand by ya.

CHRIS: Yeah, and Jimmy, me husband, didn't only have to do that – he had to lay on me as well.

EILEEN: What d'you mean?

CHRIS: As part of the tests we had to . . . you know . . . do it, then as soon as we'd finished I had to get dressed and run up the hospital.

EILEEN: You're joking!

CHRIS: My life – it's called a post coital test. Something to do with the cervix – they have to check how well the sperm travels through the canal bit. You have to present yourself at the hospital 'shortly after intercourse', (*Pause.*) I couldn't touch nothing. It was horrible – I could feel it all dribbling down me leg – you never see anyone walk so bow legged in all your life. I was doing Max Wall impressions along Whitechapel Road. It was just like having a stick of candy floss tucked down me knickers. (*Pause.*) Anyway, there was nothing wrong with the cervix, it was me tubes.

EILEEN: I wish there'd been something wrong with mine. Oh fuck, I didn't mean to say that, just one of those stupid thoughts that come into your head. I'm sorry I said that, I'm stupid, you must think I'm a thoughtless pratt . . . I just wanna go home.

Pause.

CHRIS: Here – come over here and I'll show you something. Come on. (*Pause.*) Just below me belly button. See.

EILEEN: Little scar. Hardly see it.

CHRIS: Ask me how I got it?

EILEEN: How?

CHRIS: That was something else they done. That's where they put this thing inside me to have a look at me bits and pieces – but first they had to pump up me belly with gas so that they could get the bowel and all that pushed up out the way and get a proper look at the bits that mattered. (*Pause.*) Has your dinner gone down yet – only I wouldn't like to think it's going to come back and pay us a visit. (*Pause.*) Then they put all this blue dye inside me to find out whether the fallopian tubes was blocked. (*Pause.*) Laparoscopy they call all that – sounds like something you have with a side salad don't it? Laparoscopy and dye. And I nearly did.

EILEEN: Really?

CHRIS: No, that was another joke. The next day when I went to have a wee, it all came out blue – from the dye, like. I was worried at first but then I thought, I bet the Queen can't do this. I mean, she might have blue blood in her veins . . . but blue piss – that's a bit special. And that's not all either – after a bit the gas that they'd pumped into me started coming out – I couldn't stop blowing off. It was so embarrassing, especially during visiting time. Everyone was looking at me – I had to put a pillow under me bum – muffle the sound a bit. Farting non-stop I was. Sounded like a fucking brass-band. (*Pause.*) Now I'm back again hoping they can unblock me.

EILEEN: Make yourself sound like a drain.

CHRIS: Just shows you what some people are prepared to do to experience the joys of motherhood.

EILEEN: Sorry.

CHRIS: My fault. I don't know when to stop.

EILEEN: No, it's me, I'm what's wrong. Every minute I'm here is a slap in the face for you. Everything you've been through to be able to have a child . . . and me, what I'm doing . . . stopping one, getting it sucked out of me, emptying the contents. Someone told me they flush it away, it disappears down a pan like a lump of shit. Don't that make you hate me, don't that make you want to spit in my face? (*Pause.*) Why have they put us together – it's cruel.

CHRIS: You can always go private.

EILEEN: I don't want to be here.

CHRIS: Go home then – your clothes are in the locker. Shall I get them for you? (*Taking them out.*) Here you are. Go on, get dressed and walk out – they won't mind. One less job for them to do. Go on, go home to your mum, see if it makes you feel better, solves your problem. You can start looking round Mothercare tomorrow, you'd better get someone to start knitting a little pair of booties. What you waiting for? I'll pull the screens round for you.

EILEEN: You do want to spit in my face don't you?

CHRIS: No, you silly cow, no! (*Quiet.*) Me and you have got two different needs, love. Mine doesn't shame yours, mine is my problem for me to get on with. Don't stand yours up against it and start hating yourself. We're bound to tread on each other's toes with the things we say 'cos you're in here to end a pregnancy and I'm in here because I want to start one – but they're two different needs, love. Different. Not squaring up for a fight.

EILEEN: I just want it to be over.

CHRIS: I know. You're not the only one.

NURSE *enters.*

NURSE: Something wrong?

CHRIS: What d'you mean?

NURSE: I thought I heard someone shouting. At someone else. It sounded like it was coming from in here. It was coming from in here.

CHRIS: Must have been the radio.

NURSE: The radio's not on.

CHRIS: Oh I know! It must have been when we were playing I-spy with my little eye. It got a bit heated. The game had reached a crucial stage sort of thing – the tension had mounted up. To fever pitch. Well, you know how exciting I-spy can get. It must have all boiled over. That would explain the shouting.

NURSE: Who won?

CHRIS: We don't know. You see, just as we were about to find out – you came in.

NURSE: What are these clothes doing on the bed like this?

EILEEN: That was when we was playing hunt the thimble.

NURSE: Hunt the thimble.

CHRIS: Well, we had to keep ourselves occupied, Nurse. Stop us getting bored or fed up. So I said to Eileen, 'What about a game of hunt the thimble followed by a game of I-spy.'

EILEEN: And I said, 'What a good idea. I can't wait.' (*Indicating the clothes.*) That's where we started hunting the thimble.

CHRIS: We was really enjoying ourselves. I

haven't played like that since I was a kid.

NURSE: That's very nice to know – but if you want to have a second childhood, can you have it a bit more quietly next time – there are other people here you know – some of them not feeling too well, some of them certainly not feeling in the mood to have to listen to other people amusing themselves. Loudly. If you could bear that in mind, your co-operation would be appreciated, as they say. And consideration as well, actually. All right then?

In the middle of this, CHRIS *and* EILEEN *get a fit of the giggles.*
Pause.
NURSE *is about to go out; then, turning to* EILEEN:

Oh and do you think you could put your clothes back in your locker – I'm sure you don't want them getting lost – that'd be no fun at all would it, especially seeing as that's something you seem to like having.

EILEEN: It's all right – I'll try and be responsible. (*Pause.*) This time anyway, eh?

NURSE (*emphatically*): Yes. (*Pause.*) OK then?

She goes.

CHRIS: Starchy knickers. She needs to be properly introduced.

EILEEN: What d'you mean?

CHRIS: Well, treating you as if everything she needed to know, wanted to know, was written on your wristband and in your notes.

She shouts as if the NURSE *was outside.*

Hello out there, this is Eileen. She's seventeen, lives in Bethnal Green and she's got a boyfriend named after Steve McQueen. Her mum wants her to have a white wedding, she buys George Benson records and she's worried sick about tomorrow.

EILEEN: You don't have to get angry on my behalf.

CHRIS: I know, but I do.

Later that evening.
CHRIS *in bed reading a magazine.*
EILEEN *is listening to a tape cassette.*

CHRIS: I can't pretend anymore that it's enough just to be friends . . .

EILEEN: Eh?

CHRIS: I'm coming to the rude bit in this story. They're in the bedroom. Shall I read it out to you?

EILEEN: Have I got a choice?

CHRIS: Not really, no. I'll start from the beginning again. This is the bloke talking. ' "I can't pretend anymore that it's enough just to be friends, that I don't want you in the way that a man wants a woman," he said as his mouth hovered close to her lips. "Please let me go," she said, making it sound like a very reasonable request, trying to conceal the very real desire that tormented her, but not really succeeding. His words, his voice, his touch were kindling little fires inside her; wildfires that could burn out of control if she let him continue. "You could never be just a one night stand to me Jean, an easy lay – with you it's something else altogether," he whispered, and caressed the smooth line of her jaw. A sensual heat was weakening her defences; she began to run her fingers through the vital thickness of his hair, trembling a little at the dark desire blazing in his eyes. Her skin seemed to come alive under his touch as his hands moved with a restless interest over the bareness of her shoulders. He certainly knew how to excite and she knew that she would not be the first lady to have slept in his bed; she wondered for a tiny distracted moment if she would be the last.'

EILEEN: Is that all?

CHRIS: That's all as far as the rude bit goes. New paragraph after that. Starts off 'The sun brilliantly filled up the bedroom as Jean stretched contentedly, last night still vivid, as vivid and bright as the sun that made the room glow. She listened for a while to the rhythm of his breathing and lightly kissed his shoulder till he woke. Then she said "Next time – d'you think you can take your fucking socks off?" '

EILEEN: She didn't!

CHRIS: We've come a long way from

Barbara Cartland. All the men now wear V-neck jumpers.

EILEEN: In *Photo Love* or *Jackie* sometimes the hero dies in a car crash and the girl gets all philosophical at the grave. But mostly the boy and the girl end up joking and loving each other in the last caption. Nothing messy ever happens. Everything's always tidied up.

CHRIS: In these, (*Waving the magazine.*) the sex is always out of this world and the sheets don't even get creased. No one ever wakes up with bad breath or cramp. Shall I tell you something? The first time I ever came my husband thought I was having an asthma attack. He ran to get me a glass of water, stupid sod. I had to explain to him. Evening was a bit of an anti-climax after that. I light a candle every time I have an orgasm now, I've had the same box of matches since 1974.

EILEEN: You're terrible, the things you say.

CHRIS: He thought foreplay was something to do with the way you hit a tennis racquet before I made him go out and buy one of them books – you know, with drawings of armpits and people wrapped round each other like spaghetti. One chapter in this book was called 'Taking the fear out of fellatio.' It was, honest.

EILEEN: I believe you. All what you said, cos . . . Oh nothing.

CHRIS: What?

EILEEN: Nothing. It don't matter.

CHRIS: Go on, no one else is going to hear and I won't tell anyone.

EILEEN: No, I can't.

CHRIS: Go on, be your best mate if you do. Be our little secret, just us two. You got nothing to worry about – very discreet, I am.

EILEEN: It's just that when you was talking about your husband – it reminded me of the first time I slept with Steve. We was both really nervous. I was a bit tense, d'you know what I mean? I wanted him to . . . you know . . . touch me. But he didn't know there was anything . . . to touch.

CHRIS: Did you tell him?

EILEEN: Well I said I've got . . . I've got this thing . . . this thing . . . that you're supposed to jiggle about . . . it makes me excited. Jiggle it about with your finger, I said.

CHRIS: What did he say?

EILEEN: Well, he was a bit surprised like. Then he was embarrassed . . . for not knowing about it. (*Pause.*) S'funny . . . being in here because of sex . . . and I haven't really ever got as much out of it as I think I should. Paying now . . . for the fun I've never really had anyway. (*Pause.*) When you're young you have fun. I had to come off the pill . . . made me depressed, I kept being sick. Three different kinds I tried. We weren't using anything else. Stupid.

CHRIS: All the years I'd been taking it . . . didn't know there was no need. (*Pause.*) D'you want to have a look at this . . . ?

Indicating the magazine.

EILEEN: Ta.

CHRIS: Article in there about what the royal baby is going to be called. I've been having sleepless nights worrying about that ain't you?

EILEEN: Yeah. (*Pause.*) When I found out I was pregnant, I wrote this letter . . .

CHRIS: Who to?

EILEEN: Magazine. Problem page. I wanted advice.

CHRIS: What one?

EILEEN: Cathy and Claire. Then I got angry with meself for being so dumb. I didn't send it in the end. Tore it up.

CHRIS: I thought they only published letters from girls worried about unsightly body hair and am I ready to wear a bra yet. (*Pause.*) Why didn't you tell your boyfriend as soon as you found out.

EILEEN: I had enough trouble taking it in meself without telling him. But when I did he hardly said anything – long silences and then he'd ask if I was sure. Three times he asked. He thought I might have been wrong, made a mistake. He didn't want to believe me.

CHRIS: I didn't really find out, it just gradually become more obvious.

EILEEN: When I came to the hospital from the clinic, the doctor I saw was really sarcastic. Patronising, y'know. First thing he said was. 'And how have we come to find ourselves pregnant?'

CHRIS: Maybe he'd never been told about the facts of life eh? I mean, he's only a doctor. What d'you expect?

EILEEN: He asked what me boyfriend did. When I told him he worked in the print – he said it was a cliché.

CHRIS: Didn't you say anything to him?

EILEEN: I wanted to tell him to piss off but you can't can you – you're there for their help and you're vulnerable, you're the underdog sort of thing. (*Pause.*) I had to undress and put this gown on just before he examined me. It stank. It stank of the smells and sweat of all the others that had worn it. It had never been washed. I felt so dirty. Then the position you have to be in when they grope inside you . . .

CHRIS: I know, it's even worse when you're in stirrups. You feel like you've got about as much dignity as a fucking wishbone.

EILEEN: When I got up after he'd examined me – he told me I looked terrible.

CHRIS: We'll both look very terrible tomorrow love, and you'll be in stirrups as well.

EILEEN: How d'you know?

CHRIS (*shrugs*): Sometimes I think it might be a better fate to change places with a pig strung up in a butcher's shop. (*Pause.*) I think I've been in stirrups most of me fucking life one way or another.

EILEEN: Least . . . we won't be awake. (*Pause.*) Chris.

CHRIS: What's the matter?

EILEEN: I keep . . . I keep wondering what it would be like . . . if . . . if I decided to keep it. Colour of its hair, eyes, how much it would weigh, whether it would make little fists when it cried. I do . . . I can't help it.

CHRIS: I know the feeling too well Eileen.

EILEEN: But thinking that . . . doesn't mean that really deep down I do want it?

CHRIS: No, it's natural for you to think like that.

EILEEN: But how can it be? It's natural for you – I can understand that because . . . because . . . but not me . . . it can't be natural for me. (*Pause.*) I'm in a right state – I'm sorry.

CHRIS: Stop apologising for Christ's sake.

Pause.

EILEEN: I hope it's all right for you tomorrow. Successful, like. I really do.

CHRIS: D'you know what I'd do – if it worked out tomorrow and I had a baby? What I'd really want to do the first opportunity I got – bite it's bum.

EILEEN: What?

CHRIS: Bite the baby's bum. I've always wanted to, babies bums are so little and gorgeous. But it's not the sort of thing you can do to other people's babies. I did it once to my sister's little boy – she gave me such a funny look when she saw me. Whenever I see her or other women with their children I always feel – excluded . . . set apart . . . like I don't belong. (*Pause.*) I want a child of my own whose bum has got round little cheeks that I can bite all day and all night. I wouldn't hurt it – no, never hurt it. Give it so much love. Share a bath with my own child, wash it, play games, see it stretch its arms out around my neck. (*Pause.*) And they all lived happily ever after.

EILEEN: What are the chances like – for tomorrow?

CHRIS: Between thirty and forty per cent.

EILEEN: Oh. So . . .

CHRIS: So if you want to have a bet on me wearing a smock or a maternity dress in a few months time you should cos you'd get a good price.

EILEEN: After everything you've had done to you . . . you could still be disappointed.

CHRIS: Back to square one. But while there's a chance . . .

EILEEN: It's worth it.

CHRIS: Not half. Be a mum. (*Pause.*) And barren is such an ugly word. Although they seem to say infertile a lot more nowadays.

Anyone would think they was talking about a piece of useless land, not worth anything, not good for anything. And friends and relations talk to you as though you've got a serious illness, something badly wrong that might not ever get cured. Talk to me about it in low voices, whispers. Time's running out. Thirty now. An otherwise healthy woman who can't conceive . . . The worst curse. Unnatural. Not normal. Not complete. What a shame – poor girl. But I'm not ill, I'm not unnatural. I just want something I might not be able to have. Lots of people have that trouble don't they? Everyone has that problem.

EILEEN: I think you'd make a good mum.

CHRIS: So do I.

EILEEN: But not me, not yet. I couldn't cope. I don't know anything. I'm still a girl and I don't really know anything. The furthest I've ever been is the Isle of Wight.

CHRIS: Why are you trying to justify yourself?

EILEEN: It's not just that. I know it sounds silly, but I wanna convince meself even more. Like when I hear about women, girls who burn their babies with cigarettes, tread on their chests or scald their legs, I wonder whether they're girls and women who wanted to have abortions but couldn't, or who changed their minds and decided to keep their babies. Thought they could love them, but just couldn't cope. Living on Social Security, living on the fifteenth floor, some of 'em. Feeling hopeless, helpless. A rat in a trap. Taking out their frustration. I wouldn't want to end up like that.

CHRIS: Monsters. Anyone that could do that.

EILEEN: No, not all of them. The situation they're in . . .

CHRIS: They're monsters! Animals! They should have the same done to them. (Pause.) That's not true . . . I didn't mean . . . (Pause.) . . . I just got this picture in my head . . . saw it happening . . . that sort of thing . . . hurting innocent, defenceless kids. And I lashed out, reacted without knowing what I was really doing. I didn't even mean it.

EILEEN: Like some of them.

CHRIS: Yeah. (Pause.) I had a friend. She was full of life. We used to go out together – dancing, clubs and that. She met this fellah, had two kids. She was left at home with them all day and she started to need valium and the kids started to get bruises on their faces. She weren't a monster. (Pause.) Perhaps her trouble was she couldn't afford to hire a nanny, eh? (Pause.) A woman's right to happiness, eh girl? A little bit, anyway. However it comes. (Pause.) Shall we have a party?

Inverting on her head a vomit bowl – a grey cardboard one.

EILEEN: That's what we're supposed to be sick in!

CHRIS: D'you feel sick?

EILEEN: No.

CHRIS: Well then.

CHRIS putting a bowl on EILEEN's head.

EILEEN: You're mad.

CHRIS: Drink? (*Indicating her locker.*)

EILEEN: What you got?

CHRIS: Dubonnet, Pernod, Dry Martini, Babycham. Advocaat, Gin, Bailey's and Orange Squash.

EILEEN: Oh – orange please.

CHRIS is already pouring it.

CHRIS: I'm glad you said that. Canape, vol au vent?

CHRIS offering her a grape, a sweet a Polo Mint etc.

EILEEN: Nice place you got here.

CHRIS: Functional but cosy.

EILEEN: Anyone else gonna turn up?

CHRIS: A nurse might try and gatecrash later, but we don't want troublemakers, do we?

EILEEN: All night is it?

CHRIS: No, it finishes at ten. It's the neighbours, y'know.

EILEEN: I'm sorry I'm not really dressed for it.

CHRIS: Oh don't worry about that – I said on the invitations it was casual. (Pause.)

Why don't you go and mingle.

EILEEN: Mingle? Who with?

CHRIS: Anyone you like. What's the matter – you shy? It's all right – I'll introduce you.

CHRIS *puts her glass of orange squash on the top of the locker beside the bed.*

Oh shit.

EILEEN: What's the matter?

CHRIS (*bending down*): That button that come off me nightdress before – I left it on there; I've just knocked it off.

CHRIST *getting under the bed to have a look.*

Bloody thing has rolled under here. (*She is joined by* EILEEN.)

NURSE *enters.*

NURSE: What are you two doing?

CHRIS: Digging an escape tunnel nurse, what d'you think?

NURSE: I wasn't sure what to think. As long as you're not having difficulties.

CHRIS: I've lost something.

CHRIS *and* EILEEN *emerging from under the bed.*

NURSE: Oh. (*Pause.*) I've just come to remind you that it's ten o'clock and you'll both have to turn your lights out now, OK? Also, as you probably know, you're not to eat anything eight hours before your operations, so no midnight feasts please. Not even a Polo Mint or a grape. All right? I hope you'll get back into bed as soon as you've found whatever it is you're looking for Mrs Kaye. Big day tomorrow. Sleep tight. Goodnight.

NURSE *goes.* CHRIS *and* EILEEN *getting back into bed.*

EILEEN: Be funny if you was, wouldn't it?

CHRIS: Was what?

EILEEN: Digging your way out.

CHRIS: But I've already signed the consent form.

EILEEN: Will it hurt us tomorrow? Afterwards.

CHRIS: Probably. But you might be relieved, more than in pain afterwards.

For me, the afterwards might be ten times worse than the before though.

EILEEN: If it doesn't work out?

CHRIS: Put your hat back on – it suits ya.

It is two am.
The bay is in darkness.

EILEEN: Chris. Chris – are you awake?

CHRIS: I am now.

EILEEN: I'd say sorry but you don't like me apologising, do you?

CHRIS: It's all right. I was more or less awake. Can't sleep.

EILEEN: I'm scared. Keep thinking about tomorrow.

CHRIS: I'm scared as well. S'why I can't sleep. D'you want a cuddle? Make us feel better.

EILEEN: Yeah, that's a good idea. That'd be nice. Shall I come over?

CHRIS (*putting on the light*): Well, me arms ain't long enough to reach you from here.

EILEEN: You know what I mean.

CHRIS: Come on then, we can be each other's teddy bear.

EILEEN: Is there enough room?

CHRIS: Course.

EILEEN (*getting into bed*): I wonder what the time is?

CHRIS: Must be about two. All right? That's better innit?

EILEEN: Being here has been much easier than I thought it would be – having you to talk to. I'm glad I was put in here with you.

CHRIS: You've been good company for me. In a place like this, especially with how anxious you feel, it's nice to be able to make friends with someone. Be nice if we could keep in touch.

EILEEN: Yeah, I'd like to. I really would.

CHRIS: Be a shame not to see you again, know how you're getting on.

EILEEN: And you.

CHRIS: Did you bring a pen with you?

EILEEN: What for?

CHRIS: I need something to write down our addresses and telephone numbers.

EILEEN: No, I ain't, no.

CHRIS: It's all right – I can use me eye pencil.

EILEEN: You going to do it now?

CHRIS: Well, tomorrow morning ain't going to be a very good time for remembering things like this is it?

EILEEN: No, you're right.

CHRIS: And afterwards . . . well, we don't know what's going to happen afterwards do we?

EILEEN: What d'you mean?

CHRIS: By the time I've recovered from me anaesthetic you might have gone home. (*Pause.*) Write it down here.

EILEEN: If someone had told me yesterday I was going to be in the next bed to someone who couldn't have children – I don't think I would have turned up.

CHRIS: Wouldn't have done you a lot of good though would it?

EILEEN: People can be unkind to girls like me . . .

CHRIS: They can be more than that.

EILEEN: Like that nurse. (*Pause.*) You've been so easy to talk to. Understanding sort of thing.

CHRIS: Have I? (*Pause.*) When I was eighteen, a year older than you – I went to a private clinic. Stayed overnight.

EILEEN: What for?

CHRIS: None of my family knew I was there. I was terrified – I held this lucky charm in my hand – so tightly the knuckles turned white. The room was very nice – it had a television and a telephone and the nurse bought me a cup of tea on a tray. Fifty pounds they charged. I got a sub on me wages. You went private then – even though a law had been passed a couple of years before for it to be done on the National Health, hospitals were refusing or making it very hard. Aggravation. Then there was the big risk that your family might find out. Girls who it was known had had abortions

got pointed at in the street, became notorious. It was a terrible thing. At the clinic they were mostly interested in your fifty pounds. (*Pause.*) 1970 that was – I bought a trouser suit that year, trying to look older than I was. Pale pink lipstick, black eyes. Still loved Tamla Motown – Diana Ross hadn't long left the Supremes. *Ain't No Mountain High Enough* she was singing. Jackson Five had just come out. The boy's name was Mark – I thought he was tasty because he was growing his sideburns long. He didn't want to know.

EILEEN: It's happened to you as well then?

CHRIS: Felt lonely waiting for the bus home next day. And it was so cold and I couldn't walk properly because it hurt too much. I bought a walnut whip to cheer myself up. I was sick in the kerb. Me mum thought I looked a bit peeky. Something I ate round Sharon's last night I said. Sharon was my alibi.

EILEEN: D'you regret it – because now . . .

CHRIS: Because now when I want to get pregnant I can't and when I was before I didn't want to know? No, course I don't regret it. I felt exactly the same as you do now. It wasn't a missed opportunity.

EILEEN: To hear you talking, you never sound sorry for yourself or bitter.

CHRIS: Oh I get bitter and sorry for meself. It's easy if you try. But I can make people laugh and I can make meself laugh as well – so perhaps it's harder to tell when I get like that. I s'pose you'd call it light and bitter.

EILEEN: That's terrible.

CHRIS: I know.

EILEEN: You've been honest with me. I appreciate that.

CHRIS: And you have with me, haven't you?

EILEEN: Yeah, but you also . . . like . . . when before I got upset and I said I didn't want to be here anymore. You told me what you thought. Made sense. It was good for me to hear. Being straight with me like that, treating me like . . . I don't know . . . an adult, an equal. (*Pause.*) Something I don't understand though. If you got pregnant then and you can't now – what happened in between.

CHRIS: After I'd had the dye and laper – whatever-it-is, they told me my tubes were blocked.

EILEEN: Did they say how it happened?

CHRIS: I asked them.

EILEEN: Did they tell you.

CHRIS: Yeah.

EILEEN: How?

CHRIS: How d'you think?

EILEEN: I don't know – s'why I'm asking.

CHRIS: They said it was most probably because of the termination I'd had when I was 18. Something must have caused an infection. It's called a complication.

EILEEN: Christ.

CHRIS: Funny really, I remember having a pain in my stomach for days afterwards. I didn't tell anyone though – I thought I was still getting over the operation. It went away.

EILEEN: Tch.

CHRIS: Some people would call that poetic justice, some people would say it's rough luck. I think it's fucking typical. (*Pause.*) I wasn't going to tell you and I was hoping you wouldn't ask in case it made you feel even more nervous about tomorrow. But that wouldn't have been treating you like you want to be treated. Not honest either is it?

EILEEN: Well, if it did happen to me – I just hope I could be as strong as you, and have your bottle.

Pause.

CHRIS: There's a young boy lives on our estate. He's spastic, wears calipers. When the other kids used to see him, they took the mickey, threw things at him, called him Raspberry. You know, raspberry ripple – cripple. One day, he turned round, stuck his tongue out and blew one. 'There's a raspberry', he said. I thought that was terrific. They haven't bothered him since. That's bottle, that's being strong – what he did.

EILEEN: What you saying – that we should be like him.

CHRIS: I don't mean that we actually have to go round making rude noises, but we need to have his attitude.

EILEEN: We're not raspberries though are we, we're not cripples.

CHRIS: All I know is you're in here, you're boyfriend doesn't have to be. I'm in here, my husband ain't. You're the one who had to cope with sleepless nights, you're the one who had to sort it all out and be told by your father that you disappointed him and be told by some doctor that he hopes you've learned your lesson. You're the one who has to try and walk out of here without falling over. It's me who gets made to feel like a freak, incomplete because I'm not buying Farley's Rusks. Because I've got no reason to. It's like having stones thrown at you – like the cripple boy. Like a raspberry. But we blow 'em as well, right, and stick up for ourselves. We blow 'em as well.

EILEEN *nodding; recognition.*
Pause.

EILEEN: When I go home tomorrow I'm not going to sit in me room with the curtains drawn . . .

CHRIS: D'you promise?

EILEEN: Yeah, I promise. I'm going to read a book, play me George Benson records. And . . . and . . . tell me mother to stop looking like she's just broken her best cup and saucer. (*Pause.*) I'll tell Steve to . . . you know . . . start doing it better. Get him one of those books. And I'd better go to the Health Clinic as well as see about using the cap.

CHRIS: And get in touch with us won't ya?

EILEEN: I tell you what, wouldn't it be nice if I could come round and babysit for you eventually, so you and your husband could go out.

CHRIS: No, let him babysit and me and you'll go out.

EILEEN: Yeah! (*Pause.*) I'm going to get back in me own bed now.

CHRIS: All right – go on then. Mind you don't fall arse over tit.

EILEEN: I'll try.

Pause.

Chris.

CHRIS: What?

EILEEN: Thanks.

CHRIS: Piss off.

EILEEN: See you tomorrow.

CHRIS: Yeah.

She turns the light out.

THE LUCKY ONES

The Lucky Ones was first presented at the Theatre Royal, Stratford, East London, on 19 October 1982, with the following cast:

JOE	Perry Benson
DAVE	Phil Daniels
TIMOTHY	Mark Draper
DEBBIE	Kim Taylforth
LAWRENCE	Richard Ireson

Directed by Adrian Shergold
Decor by Jenny Tiramani
Lighting by Gerry Jenkinson

Scene One

The basement of an office block, DAVE, TIMOTHY *and* JOE *are working. They are clerks.* DAVE *breaks off, looks at the other two.*

DAVE: D'you want to know what life's biggest mystery is? D'you want hear a bit of philosophy? Why is it, I often find myself wondering, that you can never get a bar of chocolate out of a vending machine? I mean, wherever I go, especially on railway platforms, I see people innocently putting their 20p's in the slot in return for a bar of whole nut. And do they get it? Do they fuck. The world is full of vending machine victims. They frown and tug at the bit that's supposed to pull out but it always seems to have been stuck with superglue or something. So naturally they try to retrieve their coins by pushing the refund button but the machine only seems to think it's been designed to swallow your money. It doesn't seem to realise it was intended to provide anyone with chocolate. Anyway, some people pluck up enough courage to give the machine a bang, but furtively – like reluctant vandals. Then they get embarrassed and go all red when other people start to look and they have to walk sheepishly away, having lost their 20p and their dignity. And their train has long since gone while they, in their idealistic and pathetically hopeful way, thought they could persuade the machine to hand over the chocolate that they've paid for. Tough tits, says the machine, I've got your money, suckers, but you ain't having my whole nuts. Some people smash the machine to bits but they get arrested. Some people are luckier and manage to negotiate a packet of Wrigleys which is not what they wanted at all, but they're thankful for whatever the machine is kind enough to let them have. I've seen people with their arms pulled out of their sockets, slumped and sobbing beside vending machines, broken by the struggle, shame and deep shock of it all. Life is like a vending machine I reckon – out of order but with no sign up to warn you.

TIMOTHY: What a profound load of shit.

JOE: You could always take down the serial number of the machine and send a letter complaining to the manufacturers. They'll have to give you your money back. Or a free bar of whole nut. Through the post. It might get squashed in your letterbox though.

DEBBIE *comes in, hangs up her coat, sits at her desk.*

DEBBIE: Bloody murder on those trains. Some bloke decided to stick his elbow in my ear all the way from Stratford to St Paul's. He weren't happy with just that though – then he tried bashing me leg with his umbrella. At least I think it was his umbrella. It's a good alibi for perverts, the rush hour, you're so squashed together you don't know whether the bloke behind you is interfering with your clothing or just trying to get off. It's horrible being that close to people – you can see the wax in their ears.

DAVE: And the blackheads in their noses. When I've got a few spare minutes, why is it . . . ?

DEBBIE: You feel like cattle being transported sometimes.

TIMOTHY: What are you – a pig or a cow?

DEBBIE: Pigs aren't cattle, Timothy old chap.

TIMOTHY: Then you must be a cow.

DEBBIE: Bulls. They're cattle.

DAVE: Ding-ding. Round two. Are you coming out for round two, Timothy? I bet you're glad you came here, Joe – you've got ringside.

TIMOTHY: I think there's been a mis-match. After all, Debbie's only a lightweight.

Pointing to her head.

DAVE: So you're black and blue then, Deb?

DEBBIE: Perhaps it compensates for the rest of their day.

TIMOTHY (*to* JOE): Debbie always likes to think that she's the victim of frustrated males. (*To* DEBBIE:) They're probably far more interested in shoving their noses in newsprint than shoving their hands up your main feature.

DAVE: All those grey chaps in their C & A suits and down below a frantic hard-on thrashing about and depraved thoughts crawling about like maggots in a bait box. Then they have to get off the train, go up the escalators and start thinking about invoices and account reference numbers. Talk about unfulfilled.

TIMOTHY: Anyway, most women like to be groped once in a while. Makes them feel wanted.

DEBBIE: And you probably think that rape is the sincerest form of flattery.

TIMOTHY: All I know is I wouldn't touch you unless I was wearing a pair of Marigold gloves.

DEBBIE: Into rubber are you then? Little fetish of yours is it? What do you use for washing up – a durex on each finger?

JOE: Thats what happens in Quadrophenia – they break into a chemist's looking for pills and one of the boys finds a big box of durex. He puts one on each finger and says from now on I ain't taking no chances. (*Pause.*) No fingerprints like. I thought it was really funny.

DAVE: What's this, what's this – did I just detect signs of life, a bit of a spark? That ain't allowed here you know – can't have anyone working here with any spirit, any fucking blood in their veins. But don't worry about it – a couple of weeks at Gulley & Co and it'll soon be wrung out of you. Any bright ideas, any youthful dreams – like dishwater down a sink. What they want here is zombies in suits.

DEBBIE: And skirts.

DAVE: The undead. Polite morons with season tickets and packed lunches. You've got to be reliable and dependable me old son, about as spontaneous as a fucking metronome.

TIMOTHY: I always used to think you had a rather large chip on your shoulder, but I was wrong, it's not a chip – it's the cross of Jesus.

JOE: Don't seem too bad, but then I only started yesterday didn't I? I just got engaged as well, so the money'll come in handy.

DAVE: You mean you're getting paid as well – fuck me, you got a good deal.

JOE: Means I can start putting something in our joint account.

DEBBIE: What's your girlfriend's name?

JOE: Sandra. (*Pause.*) Here, d'you know what a bottom drawer is?

DEBBIE: Yeah, why?

JOE: Only she says she's got to start putting things in it and when I said 'But I thought that's where you keep your jumpers,' she kicked me.

DEBBIE: Just means useful things you start collecting before you get married.

JOE: What, and you put 'em all in your bottom drawer?

DEBBIE: No! It's just a saying. (*Pause.*) I suppose you could have picked a better week to start. We'll be stuck down here for the next fortnight. It's more like a dungeon than a basement. Bit of a cheek if you ask me – first job, first day and you're sent down here. At least they could have showed you where to have a wee.

DAVE: There's only one word to describe that sort of treatment – debasement. Get it?

TIMOTHY: The lowest place in the building is very appropriate for some people I think.

JOE: That bloke showed me where the toilet was . . . and the coffee machine.

DAVE: Yeah, I'm afraid that's going to be about the size of your world here, Joe – the space between your desk, the bog and the coffee machine. And when they start talking about broadening your horizons and getting you out of the office – all they mean is getting you to take a parcel down to the post room.

JOE (*to* DEBBIE): What we're down here for – what did you say it was called?

DEBBIE: Annual review of files.

DAVE: Usually we have the whole of the outside crew of the BBC down here, to film it. It's bigger than the Cup Final, it's an event of historic importance. I piss my pants with anticipation.

DEBBIE: Can you remember any of what I said yesterday about what we have to do and why?

DAVE: Your starter for ten – no conferring.

JOE: There's three types of files – dead, dormant and live. All these files here are either dead or dormant. All the files that have been dormant for more than three years we have to make dead. And the ones that are dead have to be put in boxes for . . . for . . .

DEBBIE: Disposal. (*Pause.*) How d'you know which ones have been dormant for three years.

JOE: By the date of the last correspondence in the file. Why do you have to say correspondence – why can't you just say bit of paper?

DEBBIE: I suppose they think it sounds better.

JOE: Anyway, if the date of the last correspondence was more than three years ago, then as far as the annual thing goes . . .

TIMOTHY: Review.

JOE: They're counted as dead. Then . . . er . . . then what?

DEBBIE: The dead and disposed files have to get logged in this book. The book has got three headings. Subject, file number and date of disposal.

JOE: And where's all the live files?

DEBBIE: They're upstairs in drawers and cabinets – they're being used all the time. They're current.

TIMOTHY: I.e. live.

DAVE: There's three types of clerks as well – dead, dormant and live. They're all live to start off with, tell jokes, whistle, smile – that sort of thing. Then after a bit, they go dormant in their dim offices – all silent and timid and they keep looking up at the calender to see if their forty years are up yet. Then the permanent blank expression sets in and then . . . after a bit they're dead and their names get logged in the firm's house magazine under the heading: Gulley & Co regret to announce the death of . . . name, age, section and length of service. A few adjectives like popular, hard-working, loyal and amiable. He shall be deeply missed. They organise a collection – firm sends a wreath to next of kin. Then they get disposed of in a box. They're no longer current – that's their lot.

JOE: So you're all dormant at the moment, eh?

TIMOTHY: Not quite.

DEBBIE: Timothy's dead – only no one's noticed yet.

TIMOTHY: In Debbie's case it's harder to tell – you can't figure out whether it's rigor mortis or cheap make-up. I'd be kind and settle for rigor mortis – no one could look like that on purpose.

DEBBIE: With all due respect Timothy . . . bollocks. (*Pause.*) That bloke who brought you down here yesterday – Mr Lawrence. He'll be coming down here from time to time to see how we are getting on. He's our sort of governor.

TIMOTHY: He's more than that. He's the departmental head, actually.

DAVE: We call him Lawrence of Arabia. It's our little joke. We have jokes sometimes. He lives in Kent, but we couldn't call him Lawrence of Orpington could we? I mean it don't sound exotic enough does it? Not epic exactly. Lawrence of Orpington. Don't conjure up deserts and battles and heroic feats. More a case of gnomes in the garden and Ford Fiestas in the garage. (*Pause. Then quite viciously.*) He calls us his staff like he bought us at a fucking auction.

JOE: Is there much overtime in this job? No one said anything, but I'd be interested if there was.

DAVE: Overtime! What planet did you say you was from! I can see we're going to have trouble with you. Doing overtime here – it's like asking a drowning man if he wants a glass of water.

JOE: Well, I thought . . . time and half or something.

DAVE: They're already going to take most of your life away . . . you don't want to give 'em the rest of it. Don't let 'em have your balls, mate.

TIMOTHY: There are some people around who don't resent the fact that they're here to earn a living.

JOE: Come in handy it would – any extra money. Saving for the big day and all that. D'you know it costs £30 to hire a photographer. Photos are £50. But Sandra says you get a free wedding album thrown in. She wants the bridesmaids in pink, violet and lilac satin dresses with high frilled collars, peach skull caps, holding lily of the valley bouquets and lately she's been saying how nice I'd look in a top hat. D'you think she's joking?

DEBBIE: Only happens once though don't it?

JOE: What does?

DEBBIE: Getting married. You set a date yet?

JOE: Not till we get a mortgage. I wanna save up enough for a deposit first. Sandra works in a bank, so she can get low interest. It was her who told me to ask about the overtime.

DAVE: You won't ever see me doing overtime. I'd tell Gulley himself if I ever saw him. I'm not working myself into a peptic ulcer for their profits. I'm not giving meself a nervous breakdown to help pay for Gulley's wife to go on a fucking health farm for two weeks. I'd tell 'em to piss off on principle.

TIMOTHY: When the Fuller account was on and we worked till seven every night, what happened to your principles then – were they out visiting friends?

DAVE: But that was only because it suited me. Had an holiday to pay for didn't I? I used 'em for me own purposes. Exploit them like they do us. Cut and run son, that's what I did. But now – I wouldn't even press the lift button for Lawrence after five o'clock.

TIMOTHY: So speaks the great British worker, the voice of ambition.

DEBBIE: Whereas it's your great ambition to have a desk to yourself with drawers on either side.

TIMOTHY: And yours must be to get on a desk with someone who'll take your drawers off.

DEBBIE: Timothy, I bet the only drawers you've ever taken down have been from your mother's washing line.

DAVE (*pointedly*): Another thing you shouldn't do, Joe, is join the social club. (*Indicating* TIM.) Only mugs do that.

TIMOTHY: More jaundiced crap. What are you going to be when you grow up – a diplomat? (*To* JOE:) I can get you a membership form if you like.

JOE: What does it do?

DAVE: It has a darts match every other Wednesday in the pub across the road. That's their idea of a social club. They have it to encourage staff relations in the firm, bit of a morale boosting team spirit, all brothers under the skin. That's what we have here instead of a trade union, a fucking social club that don't organise nothing.

TIMOTHY: There's more to the social club and you know it. Anyway, what do you expect for £2 a month – a free trip to the West Indies?

JOE: Is that how much it costs to be in it?

DAVE: It costs even more to get out.

TIMOTHY (*to* JOE): Before the rats started scratching at the walls, I was about to tell you that the plan is to buy a table tennis table out of the proceeds of the raffle they've just organised and any more they need to be taken out of the subscription funds. It can be used at lunchtimes and after work and the idea is to put it on the first floor next to the first aid room.

DAVE: Len Murray has already hailed it as a great step forward in industrial democracy and the dignity of the working man. Is Gulley himself going to unveil it with a backhand smash? Fucking hell – who needs revolution when you've got a ping-pong table on the first floor? Bet you've got to bring your own bat and balls.

TIMOTHY: At least they're making an effort.

DEBBIE: They ain't doing sod all. All you've got for your money is one outing to *Midsummer Night's Dream* in Regents Park.

DAVE: Open air Shakespeare and it pissed down with rain. What're the social club saving up for next – an umbrella?

TIMOTHY: You seem to have forgotten that it was rearranged for another night. Anyway I'm sure you'll be pleased to know that the activities of the social club won't have to be such a mystery to you in future – I've told Matheson you're interested and he'll be bringing down the application form tomorrow.

DEBBIE: That's just the sort of thing you would do.

DAVE: I can't join even if I wanted to. It's a medical reason, see. I've got a weak heart and I wouldn't be able to stand all the excitement.

DEBBIE: He's not used to being out till nine o'clock at night.

DAVE: Here, I've heard that on really wild nights someone buys a packet of crisps and passes them round. Is that true? Bad enough you have to work with them old wankers, let alone socialise with 'em. What do they talk about?

DEBBIE: Haemorrhoids and double glazing probably.

TIMOTHY: We obviously need people like you then, don't we – to raise the level of conversation to things like your new blouse and the novels of Harold Robbins?

DAVE: Firm with a human face running twopenny halfpenny social club – darts matches and the promise of a ping-pong table that you've got to pay for. While Gulley and the directors go to some French restaurant where they decide important things like whether to have paté to start with or brandy to finish. From twelve to four of course. They've got their own little social club going, except it's tax deductible. And you're forking out for raffle tickets for a ping-pong table. (*To* JOE:) No, don't have nothing to do with that, Joe. Poison.

TIMOTHY: He doesn't need you to do his thinking for him. You have enough trouble thinking for yourself.

JOE: I'm usually busy most nights anyway. I go round Sandra's and we look at mail order catalogues. (*Pause. Silence.*) For towels and cutlery and stuff.

Pause.

DAVE: Whose turn is it to get the coffees?

TIMOTHY: Yours.

DAVE: Three white and one black, right?

DEBBIE: Two white and one black with and the other white, without.

TIMOTHY: I'm white with two sugars.

DAVE: Right – so it's one white with two, one white and one black with one and one white with none?

DEBBIE (*smiling*): What about the biscuits?

DAVE: Up yours – I'm an highly trained clerk – not a bleeding waitress. (*He goes.*)

Scene Two

Second day, JOE, TIMOTHY *and* DEBBIE *in the basement, working.*

JOE (*looking through a file*): What about this one? (*Showing it to* DEBBIE.) I'm not sure what I'm supposed to do.

DEBBIE: Don't know meself. Leave it to one side. I'll go and see Lawrence with it in a minute.

TIMOTHY: Show me – I'll soon tell you.

DEBBIE: Haven't you got your own work to do?

TIMOTHY: Course I have. But I've always got time for those less fortunate than myself. (*Trying to take the file from her.*)

DEBBIE: Can't you mind your own business for a change.

TIMOTHY: Temper, temper. Whose getting ratty, then? It's not your work anyway – it's Joe's – so hand it over and you'll get an answer. Or is that what you're worried about?

DEBBIE (*a tug of war with the file between* DEBBIE *and* TIM): Look – you're not getting paid commission – anyway, you'd be smug whether you was right or wrong. I'm supposed to be the one showing him what to do – if he'd wanted you to look at it, he would have asked – wouldn't you Joe?

JOE: I don't know really – I've only just started ain't I? It's going to get torn in half in a minute – then what?

TIMOTHY: Come on. I only want a little peek. The way you're acting – anyone would think you were fighting to defend your virginity. But that must be a long lost cause by now, anyway.

DEBBIE: Your arse and your mouth have both got a lot in common – shit comes out of both of them. (*Pause.*) It's got nothing to do with you.

TIMOTHY: I want to give you the benefit of my knowledge, I want to be a lighthouse in the foggy sea of your mind, a crutch for your infirm brain to lean on. Your anchor in life's ocean. Your ointment in life's sore.

DEBBIE: Let go. Let go you wanker. I'm going to ask Lawrence (*She pulls the file away from* TIM.)

TIMOTHY: Ask me. I'm here to help.

DEBBIE: I don't want your help, shithead.

TIMOTHY: Grow up.

DEBBIE: I'll fucking kick you in a minute.

TIMOTHY: You'll hurt your foot, you silly tart.

DEBBIE: Balls you creep.

TIMOTHY: Try and act like a lady. Change the habit of a lifetime.

DEBBIE: Prick.

TIMOTHY: You can have that later.

DEBBIE: Slimy bastard.

JOE: Er . . . anyone fancy a coffee?

TIMOTHY: Just tell her she's being stupid and unreasonable – it's your work for Christ's sake – she hasn't got a bloody monopoly on it.

JOE: I've only been here three days and you're fighting over me already. Wait till I tell Sandra.

TIMOTHY (*to* DEBBIE): You wouldn't know how many legs a dog has without the aid of a pocket calculator.

DEBBIE: With a bit of luck it would have one of them cocked up against you and be pissing on your trousers.

JOE: A lot of rowing goes on here, don't it? A lot of disagreements, like. Me and Sandra never row. She don't allow it.

TIMOTHY: Tell her to hand it over.

DEBBIE: Tell him to say please.

JOE: Can't we wait till Dave gets in? He'll know what to do. I ain't been here long enough to start making decisions.

TIMOTHY: Hand it over.

DEBBIE: Please.

TIMOTHY: Hand it over *s'il vous plaît.*

DEBBIE *lets go.*

TIMOTHY (*sarcastic*): No hard feelings.

DEBBIE: Really? Impotent as well as pushy. You've got my sympathies.

DAVE *comes in. He is wearing a leather jacket, Hawaii shirt, jeans and sunglasses. He is also carrying a large radio. He sits down, very casual.*

DAVE: Morning.

DEBBIE: What's this then?

DAVE: What's what?

JOE: How you're dressed.

DAVE: How I'm dressed. What d'you mean?

TIMOTHY (*contemptuously*): The clothes you're wearing.

DAVE: Oh that. I hadn't really noticed. Just put on whatever came to hand, stuck me hand in the wardrobe and pulled something out. You know how it is – seven o'clock in the morning.

JOE: You're wearing sunglasses as well.

DAVE: Am I? Oh yeah, so I am. Just a pair of shades you know. Nothing special.

TIMOTHY: What – in November?

DAVE: Well I had a heavy night last night. You know how it is.

DEBBIE: Only popstars wear sunglasses in November.

TIMOTHY: Perhaps he's been moonlighting. Doing *Top of the Pops* tonight are we? Been mobbed lately have you?

DAVE: Just a pair of polaroids available at any branch of Boots.

TIMOTHY: You look like a pimp.

DAVE: Cheers, Tim. You're such a smoothie.

TIMOTHY: I bet you got some funny looks at reception.

DAVE: Oh yeah – Stan the security man said whose that fucking freak over there, what a pervert. Castrate him, lock him up. He called the police, told them to bring their dogs and a big stick.

JOE: You don't look like you work in a stockbroker's.

DAVE: Don't I?

TIMOTHY: I expect that's the idea.

DEBBIE: I tell you who you remind me of. In those sunglasses.

DAVE: Available at any branch of Boots . . .

DEBBIE: Roy Orbison. Yeah, that's who it is. Roy Orbison.

DAVE: Leave it out Deb.

TIMOTHY (to DEBBIE): Why don't you get him to sing *Pretty Woman* to you?

DEBBIE: What about *Only the Lonely* for you?

JOE: You know why Roy Orbison wears sunglasses – cos the bright studio spotlights used to make him squint. Stage and studio lights – he couldn't look all cool and moody with a squint could he? When he first started out without the sunglasses, he used to squint all the time and it made him look funny – a bit soppy, like – so no one bought his records.

DEBBIE: It must have put him off playing his guitar as well.

JOE: Buying them sunglasses changed his life.

DEBBIE: Must have done.

JOE: Sandra likes Roy Orbison. She's got his greatest hits – volumes one and two. (*To* DAVE:) Is that who you're modelling yourself on?

DEBBIE: That's right cos he used to wear a leather jacket as well didn't he?

JOE: He still does.

DAVE: Hold up, hold on, hold your water. Can't a man change his threads without getting the Spanish inquisition.

TIMOTHY: Where's your suit?

DAVE: At home. In a heap on the bed. It didn't feel well today so I let it stay at home.

TIMOTHY: Better not let Lawrence see you like that.

DAVE: Thank you for that piece of advice, Tim old son, that bit of counsel. But I'm a big boy now and all that. Glad to see you're showing a responsible attitude on my behalf though.

TIMOTHY: When I joined here, I was told I had to dress in a way that was appropriate to the work I would be doing and the environment I would be working in.

DAVE: A fucking straight-jacket is more appropriate to this place, not a collar and tie.

DEBBIE: If you wore a straight-jacket, you wouldn't have anywhere to hold your pen.

DAVE: I'd improvise wouldn't I?

JOE: When Sandra saw me on Monday in this – she said I looked extinguished. I said don't you mean distinguished. Course not, stupid, she says, that's what you do to fires.

TIMOTHY (to DAVE): Well, don't be surprised by the stink when the shit hits the fan.

DAVE: Look it don't affect my ability to put files in boxes does it? (*Picking up a pile and throwing them in.*) See? I mean, I could understand all that petty bollocks about what's appropriate if I was a deep sea diver and I turned up on the rig in a pair of swimming trunks. But I ain't. The FT index ain't going to collapse if I don't put my tie on is it? And if the Stock Exchange ain't exactly frothing at the mouth about how I'm dressed – then why should that lot upstairs be? Will they think that I'm unstable cos I ain't wearing their uniform today. Yeah, personnel will put on my file: 'Highly psychotic and dangerous – once wore a leather jacket to work'. I wonder what else they've got on it? Lives in East London – probably has criminal tendencies. A bad risk. Unsuitable for a position of responsibility. Not promotion material.

DEBBIE: Yeah – they not only want you to look like a Burton's shop window dummy – they want you to act like one as well. (*Pause. To* JOE:) Did you know the girls here can't wear jeans or trousers – we've been told it's not feminine. Only skirts and dresses.

TIMOTHY: That's just as well – you need all the help you can get. (*Pause.*) Why don't you both go and work on a building site – you can wear what you like there.

JOE: A lot of people like dressing like this

though don't they – it makes them feel better. My grandad always liked looking smart – he asked to be buried in his best suit – but only when he was dead like. (*He starts laughing but no one else responds.*)

Pause.
He puts files on edge of DEBBIE's *desk, walks back to his own.*

DEBBIE: Have you finished with this already?

TIMOTHY: Obviously.

DEBBIE: Can't you work it out then.

TIMOTHY: I could if I felt like it.

DEBBIE: Why haven't you then? You was keen enough before. Bleeding desperate.

TIMOTHY: You'd . . . you'd better ask big chief. I'm not paid to make executive decisions.

DEBBIE: After all that performance – what a show up, what a let down. Mouth and trousers couldn't cope.

TIMOTHY: Look, if you were suffering from acute bloody migraine, you wouldn't be feeling like a million dollars, I can tell you.

DEBBIE: Is that what you've got then?

TIMOTHY: Why d'you think I couldn't deal with that? Acute bloody migraine that's why.

JOE: Sandra gets them. It's a living hell, she says, a waking nightmare. I massage her temples.

DEBBIE (*to* TIMOTHY): It came on sudden didn't it?

TIMOTHY: Acute migraines are like that.

DEBBIE (*going out with the file*): I read that they can be brought on by what you eat. And you've just had to swallow your pride haven't you?

TIMOTHY (*as* DEBBIE *goes*): Why don't you just go and . . .

Whatever TIMOTHY *is about to say should get drowned out by* DAVE *turning on the radio very loudly.*

TIMOTHY (*turning round sharply*): What the fuck is going on?

DAVE: What?

They all have to speak loudly to make themselves heard.

TIMOTHY: What the hell's this all about?

DAVE: What?

TIMOTHY: Turn that bloody thing off.

DAVE: Eh?

TIMOTHY: Turn that bloody thing off, I said.

DAVE (*turning it down*): Sorry – what was that? I couldn't hear cos I had the radio on too loud.

TIMOTHY: Have you just brought that in?

DAVE: Certainly Ollie.

JOE: Music while you work – smart! Is that Radio One?

TIMOTHY: I hope you're not figuring on having it on down here.

DAVE: That's exactly what I'm figuring.

TIMOTHY: I don't want to be tedious or anything, but it might have escaped your notice that people don't bring radios into offices. They might bring their sandwiches but they don't bring those.

DAVE: They should do. Everyone should. Be a laugh wouldn't it? Be fun.

TIMOTHY: We're not here to have fun, fun takes place outside at weekends and Bank holidays. Fun is not allowed here – it's not suitable. Neither is that radio.

DAVE: But don't you think that's sad, Tim me old son? Why does it have to be like that eh? I wanna make it different for a change. With this radio, you'll be able to sing along to all the records, you'll be able to tap your feet and drum your fingers. Better than hearing the sound of filing cabinets being opened. My mate works in a garage – they have a radio on all the time there.

TIMOTHY: You'll get us all in the shit.

DAVE: Look, this ain't even an office. It's a basement, it's soundproof – we can have this on as loud as we like – no one'll know.

TIMOTHY: I'll know.

JOE: Oh yeah, I forgot about that – it wouldn't do your acute migraine much good would it. (*To* DAVE:) Don't have it too loud – he's got acute migraine.

TIMOTHY (*to* JOE): That's very thoughtful of you but if I'd wanted my own personal shop steward I'd have asked for one – OK? (*To* DAVE:) First the outfit and now that. Are you in training to be a redcoat at Pontins or do you think you're being subversive?

DAVE: Subversive? Who me? Leave off. I'm a loyal employee – they look after me. They give me a plastic wallet for my season ticket and my security pass and they try to remember my name when I'm pissing beside them in the bog. And they tell me if I show the right attitude I might get my own phone to use in fifteen years' time. (*Pause.*) At least this radio'll remind us there's a world outside. Not just at weekends and Bank holidays but all the fucking time. Get down on it Tim. (*Loudening it up again.*)

TIMOTHY: Child.

DAVE: Wet blanket.

TIMOTHY: At school there were naughty boys like you. Except that their trick was to flick bits of paper at the teacher when her back was turned.

DAVE: Oh I never did nothing like that – I was too busy swotting for my 'O' levels so that I could have a decent career and a rosy future. And it's all been so worthwhile.

TIMOTHY: I can't work with that thing on. It just fucking disruptive.

DAVE: Stick some cotton wool in your ears then.

TIMOTHY: Stick that radio.

JOE (*to* TIMOTHY): Don't you like Radio One then? He could always change it to Capital couldn't you? Move the knob along, like.

DAVE: I'm willing to compromise.

TIMOTHY: The only knob I'm interested in him touching is the one that says off.

DAVE: I'm into on meself. On and volume.

JOE: Bit of an impasse really then innit? Clash of wills, like.

DEBBIE *re-enters*.

DEBBIE: I thought I could hear music.

TIMOTHY: So much for it being soundproof in here.

DEBBIE: Whose is that?

DAVE: Mine.

TIMOTHY: He thinks he's going to terrorise Gulley & Co with it.

DAVE: You don't mind me having it on do you?

DEBBIE: I don't but Lawrence might. He said he'd be coming down in a minute, he wants to tell us something apparently. Make an announcement. Just as well I went up there – least you got warning in advance now.

TIMOTHY: Thank you God! (*To* DAVE:) What are your plans now? After all, you're a big boy now, you can look after yourself. You don't care about what's appropriate do you?

JOE: Will you get in trouble if he sees you?

TIMOTHY: Hopefully.

DEBBIE: Shut up you. Better decide quick, Dave.

TIMOTHY: I hope he digs your threads and your tranny.

DEBBIE: He doesn't have to know about either.

TIMOTHY: Are you going to stay and defend your principles or vanish in a hurry with them up the stairs. Are you going to face the music or turn it off?

DEBBIE: He'll be down any minute. Go upstairs out of the way.

TIMOTHY: With your tail between your legs.

DEBBIE: You'll run right into him if you don't hurry up.

Fair pause.

DAVE: I'm staying.

TIMOTHY: Staying here?

DAVE: That's fucked you, innit? Put a spanner in your spokes. I'm not running away, I'm not sloping off. We don't do that sort of thing in the East End. They might be cowards in Bromley, but we stand our ground.

JOE: So you're going to meet him man to man, face to face sort of thing.

TIMOTHY: High noon.

DAVE: Not exactly.

DAVE *goes to various cabinets, checking them. He finds one and starts to get inside.*

DEBBIE: What are you doing?

DAVE: What d'you think I'm going to do? I'm staying but I won't be here – know what I mean?

DEBBIE: You're mad. You'll suffocate in there.

TIMOTHY: Fucking hell – it' like one of those silly French farces, except it's usually a wardrobe. Why don't you take your trousers off as well?

DAVE (*gets out again; to* TIMOTHY): You say anything Powers and I'll staple your balls to your trouser pockets and stick your head in the Xerox for duplicates.

DEBBIE (*smiles*): Go on, get in then. I'll make sure that it's shut.

DAVE: If he asks where I am, say I've gone for a piss.

JOE: It mustn't half be dark in there – d'you want some matches?

DAVE: What?

JOE (*shouting*): Is it dark in there?

DAVE: I don't know – I can't see. (*Pause.*) Bang on the door when he's gone.

JOE: How many times?

LAWRENCE *almost immediately pokes his head round the door.*

DEBBIE (*seeing him*): What – washing me hair you mean – three times a week.

LAWRENCE (*calling down*): Some boxes to bring down boys, if you'd be so kind. Is Dave with you?

DEBBIE: He's gone to the toilet.

LAWRENCE: Well, it should only need two of you anyway.

JOE *and* TIMOTHY *go to fetch the boxes, i.e. go up the stairs to the door which* LAWRENCE *is now holding open for them.*

(*As they pass.*) Don't forget – it's knees bent and back straight when lifting – you might not look too good in a truss. (*He shuts the door after them, comes in.*) Any traumas since you came up?

DEBBIE: No. All quiet.

LAWRENCE: Good. Good. (*Pause.*) I'm probably being very sexist by not asking you to go and do some humping with the boys, if you'll pardon the expression. In this day and age apparently women have an equal right to a hernia.

DEBBIE: Not if we lift from the knees and keep our backs straight.

LAWRENCE: True. If you know how to take weight, you'll be ready for whatever comes your way, as they say. Anyway, who am I to talk? I never do any heavy work if I can help it – I always claim managerial privilege. Makes Life easy. Can't do that at home though, no such thing as managerial privilege there.

JOE *and* TIMOTHY *come down carrying a box each.*

Just as well you're not card carrying members of ASTMS – I might have a demarcation dispute on my hands.

TIMOTHY: Because we've got muck on ours maybe, Mr Lawrence?

LAWRENCE: Quick off the blocks Tim, considering it's this early in the day.

TIMOTHY: A bowl of Rice Crispies for breakfast works wonders.

LAWRENCE: It obviously does. (*Pause.*) And what do you think of it so far, Joe?

JOE: Think of what Mr Lawrence?

DEBBIE: You're supposed to say rubbish.

JOE (*to* DEBBIE): Why?

LAWRENCE: I was talking about work actually – how are you finding the place?

JOE: Oh, it's quite easy once you get on the central line.

LAWRENCE: No – the job I mean.

JOE: Not too bad really, thanks.

LAWRENCE: Settling in OK then? Haven't had any overwhelming desires to spend large parts of the day in the bog with a *Daily Mirror* I hope.

JOE: No, everything's all right really.

LAWRENCE: If there's nothing incurably wrong, like you suddenly decide you've had a calling for the priesthood all along, or that you think you're an artist – then you'll find it pretty painless here.

JOE: No, it's all right.

LAWRENCE: Can't beat the ebullience of youth can you? Whatever happens.

JOE: Sorry?

LAWRENCE: To overcome all obstacles –
I'm sure you'll be all right. And anyway,
you've got expert tuition from Debbie
here, who I'm sure is taking you in hand
so to speak.

TIMOTHY *laughs.*

DEBBIE: Were you saying upstairs you had
an announcement to make Mr Lawrence?

LAWRENCE: You make me sound like an
MC in a strip club or the father of the
bride – I don't so much have an
announcment to make, just something to
say to you. But I'll wait till Dave honours
us with a visit.

TIMOTHY: He seems to have vanished
without trace. He was here just a minute
ago. Perhaps he's gone into hiding
somewhere.

DEBBIE (*to* LAWRENCE): He must still
be in the toilet. He had a kebab last night
– on the way home from the pub – said he
was up all night. Stomach troubles –
diarrhoea and vomitting. Bucket by his
bed. He looked really pale when he came
in this morning.

TIMOTHY: Yes, I thought he looked a bit
different this morning. Not his usual self.

LAWRENCE: Well, I don't really want to
hear his case history so I think we'll push
on. As you are no doubt aware, 1982 is
the twenty-fifth anniversary of Gulley &
Co – a sort of diamond jubilee. What you
might not know is that this year also
happens to be Mr Gulley's sixtieth
birthday – November 12th – and it's been
decided to celebrate this double event
with a presentation to him on that day – or
evening to be more precise. There's going
to be a buffet do in the conference room
and I've been asked to make the
presentation, so altogether you've got
three reasons for feeling deliriously
happy and overjoyed.

DEBBIE: Is everyone invited to the buffet?

LAWRENCE: Heads of department and
their wives only I'm afraid. But the good
news though is that on the afternoon Mr
Gulley will be unveiling a plaque on the
ground floor to commemorate the
anniversary. That's for all to come to.
(*Pause.*) Now, what's envisaged as far as
the presentation is concerned is a gift for

Mr Gulley which would be the sum total
of donations made by generous and
appreciative employees of Gulley & Co.
That means money has to be collected
and there needs to be one collector for
each floor – there are four floors and four
of you and as you're all in my department
and I'm the one making the presentation,
I don't think it takes much working out
what I'd like to happen.

DEBBIE: You want us to go and collect
money for Mr Gulley for a presentation
that no one is invited to?

LAWRENCE: Got it in one.

DEBBIE: But Joe isn't known to anyone in
the building except us – I don't think he
could really do it.

TIMOTHY: Well it might be a good way to
make himself known.

DEBBIE: What's he supposed to do – rattle
a box in someone's face and say who are
you – I want some money. (*This to*
TIMOTHY.)

LAWRENCE: If I could just call a truce
and grab your attention again. (*Pause.*) I
think Debbie's point is fair enough –
although it's something I had already
anticipated and after spending hours of
fevered mathematical calculation
consulting every major textbook in an
office strewn with bits of paper – I've
come to the conclusion that one of you
will have to do two floors.

*The sound of a radio momentarily
switched on inside one of the cabinets.
Looking at the three of them,
LAWRENCE goes to the cabinet, opens it
and finds DAVE crouched inside
clutching his radio. LAWRENCE just
looks.*

DAVE: Just looking for me pen Mr
Lawrence. I know I've dropped it in here
somewhere. Can't see properly without a
light.

LAWRENCE: Can you come out of there?
Right now. (*Pause.*) Let me guess –
you've invented a new sport – a form of
pot-holing. And instead of caves and
ropes you dive into a cabinet with a radio
dressed up like an extra from *West Side
Story*. Am I close? Or am I just groping in
the dark like you've obviously been?

DAVE: Hard to explain really Mr
Lawrence.

LAWRENCE: Try. Do.

DAVE: Well, me clothes and that . . . when I found out you was coming down. I thought it might be best if . . . if I wasn't exactly parading about.

LAWRENCE: So you hid. In there. Like a naughty child fearful of a smack from its mother.

TIMOTHY *sniggers/snorts/giggles.*

DAVE: I didn't mean to act like that. It wasn't done in that kind of spirit exactly.

LAWRENCE: Was I supposed to be the victim of a prank then, piggy in the middle of a joke everyone was in on? I take it it was done in collaboration with these three?

DAVE: No . . . they weren't involved. It was my idea.

TIMOTHY: Independent improvisation.

LAWRENCE (*to* TIMOTHY): But with your knowledge. A knowledge that none of you were anxious to pass on.

DAVE: I just thought it would have saved a lot of bother if I weren't seen. That's all.

LAWRENCE: Well on the way home in a minute with your radio to keep you company you can reflect on the fact that you are not paid to show everyone what a colourful, non-conforming individual you can be. It's just not on. If I'd wanted to employ someone to lurk inside a stationery cupboard, then on being discovered to tell me he's looking for his pen, I would have gone to a theatrical agent, or a local lunatic asylum. Wouldn't you?

DAVE: Are you saying you want me to go home and change then?

LAWRENCE: Into something less comfortable and more appropriate, please. And however long it takes you to go there and come back, you'll find the equivalent amount deducted from your pay at the end of the month. Sorry about that. You probably heard about the collection for Mr Gulley from inside there. You'll need no great deductive powers to figure out who'll be doing two floors. I do have to put my foot down sometimes. It's a pity that this time it had to be put down on your balls, but I can't allow those kind of antics. (*Pause and*

going out:) I'll let you know at some stage when I want you to go round and do your money-raising bit. See you anon. Have a safe journey David. (*He goes.*)

Pause.

DAVE: He didn't notice me sunglasses though did he? (*Pause.*) I hope me Mum's left the bathroom window open – I've forgot me key.

Scene Three

Same day, lunchtime. JOE *is sitting alone in the basement, eating his lunch. Getting up, he takes a banana out of his pocket.*

JOE (*flashing*): Cop this Sandra's mum! (*Pause.*) Not good enough for your daughter? I ain't going to marry her if she ends up looking like you. I'll stick that flower vase up your arse. Anyway, my mum says during the war you had every American soldier who came over. You'd do anything for a bar of chocolate and a pair of stockings, she said. And I tell you something else, she only wants to get married to get away from you – you've made her life a misery. Oh yeah, and the other reason is she wants to have sex all the time. Your daughter goes like a train, you know.

TIMOTHY (*having watched him through all of this*): What's wrong with you – delirium or a personality disorder?

JOE (*sheepish*): Just talking to meself . . . thinking out loud sort of thing.

TIMOTHY: Well I didn't think you'd been reciting one of Shakespeare's sonnets.

JOE: You're back early.

TIMOTHY: I haven't been out. I suppose the other two are.

JOE: Sandwich bar, yeah. Where you been then?

TIMOTHY: I've been using my free time like a good boy should – to the tune of twenty-four quid. Not a bad little investment portfolio is it? (*Holding aloft an envelope.*)

JOE: Is that how much you've collected?

TIMOTHY: 'Fraid so. Acting on behalf of my client Mr Gulley, I went out onto the floor selling shares of charm and persuasion at optimum price. Sufficient capital was raised from pockets to box and transactions completed at one-fifteen. I think I'm a born broker. Or jobber. Whatever's necessary. A dealer, anyway.

JOE: Lawrence'll be impressed won't he?

TIMOTHY: The thought had crossed my mind. He who collects most shines brightest.

JOE: You'll be in his good books.

TIMOTHY: Quite right. That'll be my commission.

JOE: Seems like you've put a lot of effort into it. Debbie and Dave don't seem all that bothered.

TIMOTHY: No, that's why when I've got a partnership, they'll still be putting bits of paper in envelopes. Yeah, when I'm helping to promote the industrial expansion of this country, they'll still be arguing about who's turn it is to get the coffees.

JOE: You've got your sights set then?

TIMOTHY: Can I ask you something? What are you here for – or what d'you think you are here for?

JOE: Well . . . steady job for a start, I suppose. Good place to be in, lot of prestige, like – people are really impressed when I tell 'em I work for a stockbroker's – and there's two sofas in the reception. Lots of prospects for getting on. Opportunities, sort of thing. That's what it said in the brochure I wrote off for anyway. And it's better than being in one of the YOP schemes.

TIMOTHY: And what did you say to Lawrence when he asked you how you were getting on?

JOE: I said it was all right.

TIMOTHY: Exactly.

JOE: What d'you mean exactly?

TIMOTHY: All right wasn't a word he wanted to hear. You sound about as enthused as someone who forgot to make a detour around a lump of shit. Thrusting young executives of tomorrow don't say all right. Great, fine, or very well thank you, was what he wanted to hear. Or

rather, what he thought you should have said.

JOE: D'you reckon?

TIMOTHY: I don't reckon, I know. What you have to do here is make yourself visible. Make yourself visible, but never be a nuisance or a bore or a threat. Be acceptable.

JOE: I don't get what you mean.

TIMOTHY: Keen but not gushing, ambitious but benign with it, responsible but with a sense of humour. A decent, healthy one of course. Jokes about Irishmen, that sort of thing. One of the lads, but not one of the lads. D'you know what I'm trying to say?

JOE: The right attitude.

TIMOTHY: The right touch. When Lawrence makes a joke, participate, but don't compete, laugh and enjoy his wit but don't threaten it with your own. When he asks you something, don't be monosyllabic, get a bloody conversation going. But make sure you let him say all the important things. Your job is just to chip in every now and again. D'you know that one of the section supervisors in claims is only twenty-five. Not a graduate entrant either. Lawrence recommended him. He's bright enough, but not exactly outstanding – but he was one of the only clerks to bring a briefcase into work with him – had nothing in it of course, except the *Daily Express* and his ham sandwiches. But he looked like he took the job seriously – and that made him visible. As well as that he was also very active in the social club – arranged a football match once between here and the Manchester branch. And that made him highly acceptable – enterprising, enthusiastic young clerk who liked normal fun things like football – at the appropriate time of course. One of the lads, but not one of the lads. Salt of the earth. That's what Lawrence obviously thought. Visible and acceptable, that's what's needed.

JOE: Is that what you wanted to be then – a section supervisor?

TIMOTHY: What I want is a recommendation from Lawrence to personnel to let me study for the broking exams. That would be right up my street,

I can tell you. Day release and course fees paid by the firm. A bloody impressive and very hard to come by qualification, and I'll be a blue button.

JOE: Blue button.

TIMOTHY: It'll give me professional status. On top of that I'll be able to choose what firms I want to work for, more or less, because I'll be a bloody rare commodity, you see. Roving brief, wandering star and all that. Even set up on my own eventually. Not to mention the countless lunches paid for by clients, and a bit of under the table speculation with the privilege of inside information. Oh yes, that's what I'm into. But to get the chance you've got to be a bit special – university background usually – but not necessarily. If Lawrence felt strongly enough . . . so if he wants us to do a collection for Gulley then I make sure I do it bloody well. You know something – I have fantasies about Lawrence collapsing and me saving him with the kiss of life. He'd be eternally grateful wouldn't he? (*Pause*.) But I suppose I wouldn't mind having to settle for section supervisor – that eventually leads to departmental head. (*Pause*.) Threadneedle Street though – that's where the money and glory is.

JOE: Least I've got me foot in the door now, that's what Sandra says. Best thing I ever did – going to college and taking 'O' levels. Applying myself. It's a right door opener innit – education. What it can do for you, like. I mean, I wouldn't be working here if they didn't think I was going to be an asset to 'em would I? Recognised me potential, like.

TIMOTHY: Whenever you clap eyes on anyone you don't know but who are over thirty and wearing a decent suit – smile at them, say hello. Even hold the door open for them sometimes. Don't overdo it though – don't be a creep, be pleasant. Like I said, the right touch. They're invariably going to be more important than you and you need all the allies you can get here. The more people you're on first name terms or any name terms with, the better.

JOE: I've got the chance now to make the most of me abilities. Better meself. I'm the only male in my family that's ever got a job in an office, my dad's a bus driver – that's about all he can do, he says. He's well pleased with me.

TIMOTHY: I wonder how much the other two have collected. I bet between them it still doesn't come near £24.

JOE: A rewarding career and a bright future – that's what they told me in the interview. And what's that other word – that sounds like someone sneezing. Oh yeah. Initiative. Never be afraid to use it.

TIMOTHY: I think I'll trip upstairs to Lawrence this afternoon. Hand over the cash. First past the post and all that. *N'est ce pas*?

JOE: It's funny but when I'm standing on the platform with all the other commuters and I'm reading me paper, I feel . . . sort of . . . you know . . . grown-up. But it's true in a way innit – I'm a young adult now. I'm working and that. The bloke on the door even calls me sir, I really like that.

TIMOTHY: He's bound to wonder why the other two haven't been so diligent – something badly lacking in their attitude he might think. Another gold star in my exercise book, a black mark in theirs. I might even send old Gulley a birthday card – a personal greeting. No, that's too obvious. (*Pause*.) What about a small, tasteful congratulations card for twenty-five years. Low key but sincere. The right touch. May the future be as fruitful. Best wishes – Timothy Powers. Nice one.

JOE: No, I'm not a kid anymore – that's definitely true. New era now. National Insurance contributions, season ticket, responsibility. Sandra said she became a woman when we got engaged. Before that, she reckons, she was just a simple girl.

TIMOTHY: I hope that you've gathered there's more to working here than just doing your job. I'm only telling you all this cos you seem like a good bloke and I thought you might appreciate someone like me passing on what he knows. Little pearls . . . But you'll have to earn your own public relations diploma – you can't borrow mine. (*Pause*.) I'm . . . er . . . just off to the card shop. If the others come back, where I've gone and why'll be our little secret, OK. I know I can trust you –

we're blood brothers now almost, aren't we? Who knows, I might even give you a job in my firm one day. How's that for an incentive?

JOE (*as* TIMOTHY *goes out*): Just had a thought – it must have done my credit rating a lot of good – being here. Sandra wants to buy a washing machine on HP see.

Scene Four

Later on in the afternoon. JOE *and* DEBBIE *are in the basement, working.* DAVE *comes in quickly.*

DEBBIE: Has he found out yet?

DAVE: No. Sssh. Just keep a straight face.

After a few moments TIMOTHY *enters. Stuck on the back of his jacket (which should be light grey) are a matching set of bra and knickers.*

TIMOTHY: OK. Very funny.

DAVE: What?

TIMOTHY: Joke's over I think.

DEBBIE: Beg your pardon?

TIMOTHY: I've inspected the bog, the second floor and the stairwell – I didn't even find a ten pence piece. I've shot around enough to make a blue-arsed fly green with envy. I left it here, I know I did.

DEBBIE: What are you insinuating?

TIMOTHY: I'm not insinuating fuck all – I'm accusing you bastards. I never mislay things. I am not the careless type – certainly not when it comes to money. No way. You must take me for some kind of pillock.

DEBBIE: Who us? Never.

TIMOTHY: Do I look as if I walk around with an 'L' plate on my back or something?

DEBBIE: Not an 'L' plate exactly, no. Spoil your suit if you did wouldn't it?

TIMOTHY: Where is it?

DAVE: Where's that?

TIMOTHY: The fucking Taj Mahal what d'you think?

DAVE: Look – if you've lost your collection money don't go pointing the finger at us. It's not our fault if you're stupid and irresponsible.

TIMOTHY: Don't give me that shit.

DEBBIE: You're getting your knickers in a twist.

DAVE: It's a bit rich when you think about it though innit? I mean, here we are working for a firm that 'mobilises' millions of pounds into securities, oiling the wheels of investment for multinational corporations, high finance up to our eyeballs and old Tim here can't even be trusted with a measly fucking twenty-four nicker stuffed in a brown envelope. Unreliable behaviour with company funds – that ain't the stuff that thrusting young executives are made of.

TIMOTHY: How come you know how much it was then?

DEBBIE: 'Cos you kept boasting about it. (*Pause.*) I wonder what Lawrence is going to say – you've let him down, badly. He'll be very disappointed with you – grave doubts about your ability. He'll probably think you've spent the money on yourself.

DAVE: Bought yourself a new outfit. (*Pause.*) Splashed out on a change of image.

DEBBIE (*giggles*): I don't think much of your colour scheme though. (*Pause.*) Is that a spare set – for emergencies. Bit like having a spare tyre in the boot, in case you get a flat.

TIMOTHY: I don't know what the fuck either of you two are talking about, but you seem to be enjoying yourselves. This is exactly what I've come to expect from you pair of adolescent wankers. If anyone does anything that makes you feel inadequate you try to fuck it up. Your only contribution to anything you can't cope with is to take the piss. D'you know what the clinical term for that condition is? Do you?

DAVE: No. Tell us. Go on.

TIMOTHY: It's known as jealousy. Ever heard of it, does it sound familiar? What it boils down to is the fact that you didn't collect a bent washer between you and I got £24. Gets right up your nostrils doesn't it?

DAVE: You've underestimated us me old cocker – you've made a ricket.

TIMOTHY: You didn't even raise a smile.

DAVE: I'm afraid you've been badly misinformed. Our pockets are what you call bulging, our cup runneth over . . . Sullivan in computer services was so anxious to contribute as much as he could, he was thinking about taking out a second mortgage on his house in Billericay. And Childs, the section supervisor in new business, kept apologising cos he could only give me a fiver. 'Take my wedding ring,' he kept saying. And everyone I went to thanked me. Can you believe it? Thanked me for taking their dough. 'Cheers,' they all said. 'Cheers.' I was so overwhelmed I can tell you. All I was asked to get was a token of their goodwill and appreciation. What a bunch of Uriah Heeps I thought in my ignorance. What a shower of crawl up the arse jobs. But then it dawned on me – loyalty and respect. That's what it was all about. Everywhere I went on my little errand – a moving demonstration of loyalty and respect for the firm that's been so good to them. Deb can tell you it was the same story on her floor. We had to hire Securicor to accompany us along the corridors and down the stairs. I was even thinking of running off to Rio de Janiero with mine, I'm ashamed to admit. So what I'm saying, Tim old son, with this collection business is – that if it had been a league table, you'd have been relegated.

DEBBIE: I tell you what though – seeing as you haven't got nothing – why don't we give you a couple of quid out of what we collected. We don't mind doing a colleague a favour do we, Dave?

DAVE: No, of course not. A friend in need and all that.

TIMOTHY: You vindictive bastards. I'm warning you – you'd better stop this pratting about. After all, theft is a matter for the police. They'd have to be informed, right?

DEBBIE: That's not very nice is it? Who's being vindictive now? I was only offering you a bit of help. That's really upset me – being accused of stealing someone else's money after all the effort I put into going round.

TIMOTHY: Yes, it must be quite an achievement seeing as you spend most of the time off sick. I hear your GP is writing a comic novel – based on your medical certificates. How did you fit it into your schedule? I mean, what with pre-menstrual tension, post-menstrual depression and period pains, it's a wonder you can spare the time to come in at all.

JOE: Did you hear about the woman on her menstrual cycle – she came in second in the Tour de France. (*Pause.*) Just thought I'd try a little joke – to defuse the situation, like.

TIMOTHY: I'm going to the bog. When I come back I want to see twenty-four quid on that chair. If it's not, you'll be sorry. I mean it.

DAVE: He's threatening us.

DEBBIE: Don't you think you'd better change your underwear before you go out. You look like a kleptomaniac who's just run out of the launderette. You don't want people talking about you behind your back.

DAVE: Or pointing at it.

TIMOTHY: I'm sure your private little joke is highly hilarious – but you'll be smiling on the other side of your . . .

TIMOTHY *has taken off his jacket, sees the bra etc.*

DEBBIE: We tried to get you some Janet Reger but they didn't have your size.

TIMOTHY: How long have these been on here?

They don't respond, just laugh.

DAVE: Reason why it was bra and pants is cos we couldn't decide whether you were a tit or a twat. They was me sister's – don't fit her anymore.

DEBBIE: They suit you though.

DAVE: She was going to give 'em to the boy scouts for one of their jumble sales. But I thought I'd bring 'em in – have a laugh. You've been walking round like that most of the afternoon. Didn't you notice people falling off their chairs laughing when you walked past? Didn't you see the tears streaming down their cheeks?

TIMOTHY: Did you have anything to do with this? (*To* JOE.)

JOE: No, I was just a bystander. An onlooker sort of thing.

DAVE: We knew you'd see the funny side of it, Tim.

TIM *goes to the fire hose on the wall and pulls it out.*

I mean, you shouldn't be working here if you can't take a joke – ain't that right Tim?

TIMOTHY: Unless you fuckers want the contents of this in your general direction, you better forget your little prank ever started. (*He shouts:*) I'm not joking!

DAVE (*raising his arms*): Oh fuck me – it's a stick up.

DEBBIE (*doing the same*): Don't shoot – I can't swim.

TIMOTHY: Don't push it – I'm just in the mood to use this thing.

DAVE: But there ain't a fire, Tim.

TIMOTHY: Just hand over the fucking money.

DEBBIE: Stand and deliver.

DAVE: Do you accept Barclaycard Mr Turpin?

TIMOTHY: I hope you're feeling thirsty.

DAVE: Be nice if we had some scotch to go with it.

DEBBIE: Do we need our cups?

TIMOTHY: No, just some towels. Be the nearest thing you get to having a bath, won't it?

JOE: It's funny innit – I've always wanted to have a go of one of them. I've never had the chance to be in a fire yet though. I wanted to be a fireman – but I didn't have a 38 inch chest. That's what you need. The careers officer told me that.

DAVE: You don't really think we'd take the proceeds of your whip-round for Mr Gulley and then hide it somewhere do you, Tim? That'd be too unfair for words. Despicable, I'd say. Right out of order. We wouldn't mess about with something as important and worthwhile as that. I'm sure it'll turn up somewhere. Perhaps someone's handed it in at the reception. Lost property, like. And as for what you said about us being jealous – that's just silly. We admire you don't we Deb? We look up to you – you're so responsible and conscientious. Ain't that right Deb?

DEBBIE: Course.

DAVE: We don't bear no malice, I swear. My word is my bond as we say in the Stock Exchange. *Dictum meum pactum.*

TIMOTHY: Balls – I don't think someone like you is in a position to start patronising me. You're a toe-rag and you always will be because you think like one. Everything's a joke, a laugh to you – at least I've got some fucking vision. Well, the big wide world is a serious business run by adults and if you just want to ponce around then you'd better start getting used to being that toe-rag I was talking about.

DAVE: If you've got so much maturity and vision how comes you're threatening us with a fire extinguisher.

TIMOTHY: The sooner I get what's mine, the sooner we can go home. Or we can stay for as long as it takes – all fucking night if needs be. It's up to you.

JOE (*looking at his watch*): I'll have to be shooting off in a minute. I've gotta be round Sandra's by seven. She said she wants to squeeze some of me blackheads out.

DAVE: Do us a favour, Joe, you've put me off my tea now. (*Pause. To* TIM:) Tell you what, I'll prove that I'm innocent. You can search me. Come on. Or would you rather I was spread against the wall like in *Kojak* – like this, look. (*Doing so.*)

JOE: They call it frisking over there.

DEBBIE (*to* TIMOTHY): That's fair innit?

TIMOTHY: Give you something to get excited about wouldn't it? Waiting for your turn. You need a cold shower – (*Shouting.*) – and that's what you're both going to fucking get if you try and make a pratt out of me much longer! (*Quieter.*) All I have to do is turn this nozzle and bingo.

DAVE, *near the light switch, turns it off.*

Where are you, you sly bastards?

JOE: Has someone turned the lights out?

TIMOTHY: I'll get back at you for this I swear I will.

TIM *finds the switch. DEB and DAVE have both gone. He runs after them.*

Fucking pair of shits!

JOE *is left alone. He picks up an envelope that is lying on the floor.*

JOE (*shouts*): Someone's dropped something!

Looking inside, he starts taking out money. He counts it.

Timothy! Oi Tim!

JOE *goes after* TIM.

Scene Five

DAVE, JOE, DEBBIE *and* TIM *are in the middle of a conversation.*

DAVE: Well, it's a fucking liberty if you ask me. Talk about wringing out the last few drops. He'll come down and give us a fitting for a ball and chain next. First we have to do a collection for a presentation we ain't even invited to . . .

TIMOTHY: You're invited now . . .

DAVE: What – as a barman – fixing gin and tonics for our poxy senior management and their wives so's they can have a jolly fine evening at our expense? More ice please young man. Don't you work here as the lift attendant or something? Very nice little turn out wouldn't you say? Cheers. I'd rather be a fucking store detective for War on Want sometimes, I tell you.

TIMOTHY: At least you'll be there. None of the other clerks will be.

DEBBIE: It wasn't exactly RSVP with gold lettering though, was it? Not a hint of you are cordially invited, Mr Gulley requests the pleasure of your company. Wasn't even would you, could you, please, I'd be grateful. No nothing like that. Quick visit five o'clock last night to inform us that he wants us to wait on them hand and foot. Only his euphemism was giving our assistance. Token mention of his appreciation.

TIMOTHY: And a not so token mention that we'd be getting paid for it.

DEBBIE: Ever heard of that old-fashioned cliché called the principle of the thing.

DAVE: It ain't even time and a half.

JOE: I need all the money I can get hold of at the moment, Sandra says that for the honeymoon she wants to go to Tenerife. And the reception's going to be a four course sit-down with wine included, followed by a group – spot prizes, special requests and me and Sandra out on the floor for the first dance. (*Pause.*) They might give us a tip or something. Like when they have a whip-round for the coach driver.

DAVE: What coach driver?

JOE: Well, generally like. On the way back from wherever you've been. After the singing.

DAVE: Singing?

JOE: Yeah, *When the Saints Go Marching In.* (*Pause.*) All together. (*Pause.*) Might be like that next week.

DAVE: Oh yeah – I can just see it now. We'll all get together in a big circle at the end of the evening and do the hokey-kokey.

Pause.

We don't want tipping – we want our self-respect.

DEBBIE: Won't get much of that when you're having to ask some old berk's wife if she'd like a cherry in her advocaat or coleslaw with her chicken leg.

TIMOTHY: What are you going to do then – stop watering the office plants in protest, set fire to the blotting paper and call it industrial espionage or write a letter of complaint to the staff magazine? Maybe you'll get some placards and march up and down outside Lawrence's office.

DAVE (*going deliberately over the top to compete with* TIM *and hopefully bait him*): Yeah, we're going on a go-slow; black the work, withdraw our good-will, picket the stationery cupboard and the executive bog, stand by our entitlements. We're not going to stand for it. In other words, Tim old fruit, we're going to say no. In big letters. Is that simple enough for you?

TIMOTHY: I'll hold your coat. (*Pause.*) If one isn't there next week, one is invisible. Not sensible at all. Getting noticed is. Very.

DEBBIE: Like a pet dog gets noticed.

TIMOTHY: Pet dogs get fed. Stray ones get put down.

DAVE: Timothy – don't be a bottle job, a wash out, a wally. Don't be the vulture's pickings, the dog's dinner. Know your rights. Don't let your rights go out of the window for the sake of a pat on the head. Dignity. Solidarity. Victory. Stand up and speak out.

LAWRENCE *has appeared at the door unnoticed at the end of* DAVE's *speech.*

LAWRENCE: Stirring stuff David. When's the battle taking place. Agincourt?

DAVE: I . . . er . . . I was just giving Tim a bit of advice Mr Lawrence – useful tips when buying your Christmas turkey.

LAWRENCE: Really. I've just bought this down for next week. (*It is a bar steward's white jacket.*) Could only get hold of one for the time being. I don't know which one of you it'll fit. But you'll be properly kitted out in the end. Don't worry about that.

TIMOTHY: Dave – I don't know if it's slipped your sieve-like mind at all – but didn't you have a few queries about next week.

Pause.

LAWRENCE: I'm all ears, as Prince Charles would say.

DAVE: Well . . . the presentation in the evening . . . the function . . . you want us . . . me to work behind the bar . . . serving.

LAWRENCE: I still do. An expert on drink such as yourself is going to be indispensable.

DAVE: And Debbie supervising the buffet.

LAWRENCE: A running cold buffet of cooked hams, chicken breast, silverside, home made quiche, various salad mixes, even one with walnuts in it, chicken liver paté, garlic paté, a full selection of cheeses, smoked salmon – Canadian – canapes, potted shrimps, avocado prawn, smoked mackerel, trout, cheese dip, fresh cream gateaux and the perennial sausage rolls. Lots of lovely dishes and I'm sure you'll be the loveliest, Debbie. (*Pause.*) You'll be free to take home with you whatever's left.

DAVE: I think, you see . . .

LAWRENCE (*interrupting*): Not getting butterflies or cement mixers or whatever are you? There aren't many that I could trust enough to put on the front line so to speak. I'm sure you'll do justice to the occasion. I know you will. And as far as the etiquette business goes . . .

DAVE: Something else . . . I wanted to talk about, Mr Lawrence. Me and Debbie . . . I don't know about Joe . . . was thinking, not just thinking, saying as well . . . didn't think it was . . . the idea of doing . . . didn't seem what we would have decided . . . for us, I mean ourselves . . . on our own, of our own accord . . . the presentation . . . in the evening . . . agreeing . . .

LAWRENCE: I'm afraid you're making about as much sense as a drunken polar bear.

DAVE: Our job . . . working here . . . it's different . . . that's all we do . . . supposed to . . . normally. What we've been asked that night . . . not the same as what's normal . . . supposed to be working here . . . not the same.

LAWRENCE: You've got a bogey on the side of your nose, David.

TIMOTHY *laughs.*

LAWRENCE: Only joking. Now what was all that again – you must think I'm terribly slow on the uptake, I think my ears might be full of wax. (*Proffering the side of his head to* DAVID.) Can you see anything? And I hope you're not going to say you can see out through to the other side. Either I'm not listening or you're not communicating. Which d'you think?

DAVE: What I meant to say Mr Lawrence . . . about what you want . . .

DEBBIE: We don't want to work as waiters and waitresses next Thursday. We don't think it's fair.

TIMOTHY: Don't include me in that.

Pause.

LAWRENCE: Looks like . . . we've got an insurrection. A mutiny on board. Am I the one you've decided to make walk the plank or what?

Pause – no response.

Bone of contention seems to concern you're appreciation of the conception of what's fair – that right?

DEBBIE: Wouldn't it be possible for you to get someone else to do it Mr Lawrence?

LAWRENCE: More waiters and waitresses you mean? (*Pause.*) On the registers of numerous employment agencies – experienced, efficient, trained professional and eminently suitable. But I wanted something much more than that, you see. I thought there was a better way, I really did. To my mind there's a very large distinction between yourselves and the waiters and waitress you thought you were going to be next Thursday. For a start, you were asked for, wanted – very much so. Because I knew you wouldn't let me down, I knew you'd be a credit to me the department and yourselves. It was a vote of confidence with the best will in the world – not a case of who can we rope in. And that's important for me to make you understand that your presence there is going to be more than just a functional one. If you thought you were just being asked to turn up to pass the peanuts and pour the gin, then I'd be very disappointed in your estimation of me and what I'm about. It wouldn't be fair, to use your word.

DEBBIE: What else will we be there for then, Mr Lawrence?

LAWRENCE: Well, on a practical level of course you would be helping to make the evening a success, as you help to make the firm a success, by working here. I don't normally go in for platitudes, but you are part of a team here, albeit junior members of that team. So wouldn't it be nice if that sense of being part of the firm, of the team, could be reflected in your helping to muck in on Thursday? A symbol of the kind of spirit we try to engender here of people working together, for each other. Next week will be a celebration of twenty-five years of that spirit. Your refusing to co-operate would sour it. An extra-curricular contribution to Gulley and Co, rather than your normal nine to five one. And I think Mr Gulley is entitled to some small measure of appreciation. After all, he does pay our wages. (*Pause.*) Of course no one is holding a gun to your head or threatening you with thirty lashes for

insubordination. This is England, 1982. But probationary reports and promotion markings don't write themselves you know. Attitude – that's the thing.

DEBBIE: We're not trying to sabotage the evening Mr Lawrence or insult Mr Gulley, I thought the collection would have proved that.

LAWRENCE: But I suppose it just goes against your religious beliefs to have anything to do with the firm after five o'clock, to be helpful and approachable only when it says so in your contract of employment.

TIMOTHY: I'm quite looking forward to it myself. I won't be washing my hair that night or watching *Crossroads*.

DEBBIE: We won't be there on an equal basis will we?

LAWRENCE: So what's new – you're not here on an equal basis five days a week. Anyway. I thought I'd explained that aspect of it just now. When you go into a shop – do you think the person giving you your newspaper or mascara or box of tampons or whatever is some form of inferior species? Of course you don't – unless your sensibilities are warped. (*Pause.*) OK – so you're not being asked to indulge in dry sherries and the joys of social intercourse but neither are you going to be treated like Millwall supporters with syphilis.

TIMOTHY: Sweating in the engine room as opposed to standing on the deck.

DEBBIE: The point is though Mr Lawrence – we'll just be there to help other people enjoy themselves and clear up after 'em when they've finished. They'll be no celebration of the firm's anniversary for us – not a proper one anyway. Being an integral part of the spirit of the whole occasion. I mean, it sounds very nice – but it's hard for us, me anyway – to appreciate. It seems a bit like that fairy story about admiring the king's new clothes. You know the one where he ain't wearing nothing at all.

JOE: Danny Kaye sung a song about it.

DEBBIE: You see, I always thought that joining in meant . . . well, what it sounds like . . . joining in.

LAWRENCE: Well, I don't think we need

to make a philosophical issue out of it – or create a maze of excuses. The question remains – either you want to be constructive or you don't. Abuse my trust or vindicate it. (*Pause.*) You're being very silent David – seen your reservations put into legitimate perspective now have you? Yes? No? Don't know?

DAVE: What Debbie said . . . a lot in common with that. Not the same as not caring though. I think I might be baby-sitting for me sister next Thursday. She lives in Ilford. I have to get a 25 from Stratford.

LAWRENCE: I would really like to go away from here feeling that apart from Tim there was some kind of commitment and interest that went beyond salary – which I think is due for review next month, is it not? (*Pause.*) What about Joe – prepared to put yourself out, start off on the right note and show me that the firm's taken on a winner?

JOE: No, I don't mind actually. Broaden my working experience won't it and . . . help me develop me office skills . . . like communication . . . in a social environment. Showing the right attitude – be an asset like. Only thing is though – I'm a bit accident prone. Last do I went to I got an olive stuck up me nose. That was just before I opened this bottle of Pomagne – the cork hit this woman right in the eye, made her false teeth fall out . . . into the coleslaw. I had to leave early. I'm sure I'll be all right next Thursday though.

LAWRENCE: How reassuring. Remember earlier on you were talking about what's fair. Would your definition of fair include the use of the democratic process, abiding by the majority decision for the good of the community and all that. Would it?

DAVE *and* DEBBIE *both shrug, nod.*

Funny you should say that because if I've got my sums right and a fair and democratic vote took place, it would be two against two with me having the casting vote and consequently next Thursday would be graced by both your presences.

DEBBIE: We also believe in freedom of choice Mr Lawrence.

LAWRENCE: Let me put your freedom of choice into perspective. I was talking about this being England, 1982. Last week, personnel had 250 applications for two vacant clerical posts they advertised. Amazing isn't it? Steady, decent jobs are rare things today. You're in very fortunate positions, you're what's known as the lucky ones. Plenty of people anxious to be where you are now, to push you off the perch. 250. 250 applications for two posts. Employers have freedom of choice at the moment – bags of it. (*Pause.*) Having a job today, especially for young people – well, it's like having a life raft to hold onto in a very cold, hostile sea – something to cling onto desperately. Only fools would want to do something that might jeopardise their tenuous grip on the life raft, see their fingers being prised away and find themselves stranded in an ocean of nothing. An ocean of unemployment. An there'd be nowhere else to go believe me – not even for bright, young sparks like yourselves. Sobering thought isn't it? And of course that makes it so much more crucial that you please your employers. You'd do well to bear that in mind and start looking over your shoulders. Let me know when you've seen the light. Cheers.

He goes out.

DAVE: Happy birthday Gulley & Co.

TIMOTHY (*who has put on the bar steward's jacket*): How's it look?

DEBBIE: Looks like trouble.

Scene Six

A week later. TIM, JOE, DEBBIE and DAVE *are in the basement, blowing up balloons.*

DAVE: When Gulley unveils that plaque tomorrow afternoon, he's going to get a shock, I tell ya. There won't be no inscription referring to the history of his firm. He's going to find a suitable message engraved to commemorate my history in the firm.

DEBBIE: It'll put him off his speech if he reads something like 'David Shell Fuck Off 1978-1982'.

DAVE: I'd have to be anonymous though . . . know your enemy but don't let 'em spot you. Tactics of guerrilla warfare innit . . . ?

TIMOTHY: Tactics of someone who's never managed to put his actions where his mouth was, more like.

DAVE: Well right now my mouth is busily engaged in putting air into these fucking things.

DEBBIE: I knew he'd do something like this – to get his own back. He'll probably get us to butter the bread tomorrow.

TIMOTHY: Yes, it's rebounded on you with poetic justice, hasn't it?

DEBBIE: You're having to do it as well. That's some consolation anyway.

TIMOTHY: Yes, but I'm doing it as someone who's entering into the swing of things, not as someone who thinks it's some kind of punishment or revenge. I'm co-operating as Lawrence said, I'm someone whose interest and commitment goes beyond considerations of inconvenience and salary. Anyway, you can't have a festive occasion without balloons, so keep puffing away.

DEBBIE: Why are we having to do this down here anyway – what's wrong with the conference room – seeing as that's where they're going to be put?

TIMOTHY: We're not allowed in the conference room, you know that.

DEBBIE: You'll be allowed in there tomorrow night though, won't you – as a waiter.

DAVE: Why us anyway? He's got other staff – have they only got one lung each or something?

TIMOTHY: We're out of the way here in case you hadn't noticed. Not under anyone's feet. (*Getting up, on his way out.*) But next week you'll be able to surface again – like the creature from the black lagoon and frighten all human beings upstairs. (*He goes out.*)

DAVE: This is what I think of it all. (*He lets go of the two blown up balloons and watches them flying about releasing their air.*)

DEBBIE: I would have thought that lot upstairs would reckon that balloons were too vulgar and common for a do like tomorrow.

DAVE: Salad with walnuts in it . . . too much.

JOE (*holding a limp balloon, a long shaped one*): I used one of these as a contraceptive once.

DAVE: Yeah, I reckon. What d'you do with it afterwards – blow it up and have a party?

JOE: I did honest. It was a yellow one.

DEBBIE: What – were you and Sandra economising then?

JOE: No – it was just that I was too embarrassed to go in the chemists and ask for . . . you know . . . durex. So I went and bought a packet of balloons.

DEBBIE: If you used a balloon for that – I bet your Christmas decorations are something to see then.

Pause.

DAVE (*blowing up another balloon*): Now you know what it means to be an asset to the firm Joe, part of the team.

JOE: I wonder where Timothy's gone.

DAVE: Probably in the bog rehearsing his conversation for tomorrow. Learning it off by heart. Jokes, compliments, pleasantries to try out, set phrases to impress and ingratiate, like I certainly can, I surely will, with pleasure, don't mention it.

DEBBIE: Then there's words like basically.

DAVE: Generally.

DEBBIE: Actually.

DAVE: Moreover.

DEBBIE: Nonetheless.

JOE: Ants.

DAVE: What?

JOE: Ants. You know. Antsforth.

DAVE: Oh yeah. Right (*Going beside the door with two blown-up balloons*): I hope our mate Tim hasn't got a weak heart or a nervous disposition. Otherwise, it'll be a brown trouser job.

JOE: What d'you mean?

DAVE: Involuntary bowel movements. A surprise package in his Y-fronts.

JOE: Eh?

DAVE: Number ones.

As the door opens, DAVE *jumps out bursting both balloons and shouting 'bottle!'*
It is LAWRENCE, *not* TIMOTHY.

LAWRENCE: Hello to you, too.

DAVE: Oh. (*Pause.*) Sorry.

LAWRENCE: Me too.

DAVE: Er . . . er . . . I was trying to cure Timothy's hiccoughs, Mr Lawrence. He's had hiccoughs all day you see and I was just trying to help him out. Give him a shock sort of thing, when he . . . when he . . . wasn't expecting it. But you . . . er I wasn't . . . .

LAWRENCE: But I turned up instead . . . and now you've ruined two perfectly good balloons.

DAVE: Er . . . yeah. Sorry about that.

LAWRENCE: Why is it that every time I see you you're behaving like a psychopath?

DAVE: I'm sorry if I've given you the wrong impression Mr Lawrence.

LAWRENCE: You see, I think I'm at the stage now where I need to be convinced you've got a future here. I've never been in charge of a potential axe murderer before – they didn't cover that in the management courses I went on and it might be a bit of a problem. Unfortunate incidents and so on. Blood stains are very hard to remove. You know murder. And then there's the mutilated bodies to consider – and the staff replacements of course. What would I write in your annual report – 'has a disappointing tendency to hack people to death'? Not to mention the frothing at the mouth. (*Pause.*) I should imagine it's almost as bad as having selfish, unco-operative people on your staff. People who can't be bothered to join in.

Pause.

I came down here to say that some tables and chairs need shifting from the conference room. To make space for tomorrow. Your services are required.

TIM *enters.*

LAWRENCE: How's the hiccoughs?

TIMOTHY: Sorry?

LAWRENCE: David was telling me about your hiccoughs.

TIMOTHY: I haven't had hiccoughs for years Mr Lawrence.

LAWRENCE: He hasn't had hiccoughs for years David, what d'you make of that? I'll tell you what I make of it – I think someone needs to make amends don't you?

JOE: Shall I bring some of my records in tomorrow Mr Lawrence?

Scene Seven

The day of the presentation. DAVE *is sitting alone in the basement.*
DEBBIE *comes in.*

DAVE: What's happening?

DEBBIE: Mr Gulley's just unveiled the plaque – he's making a speech.

DAVE: How thrilling. I think I'll take a valium. To calm down, like.

DEBBIE: Timothy's standing up the front to make sure he can be seen clapping the loudest.

DAVE: In difficult times such as these one is made even more aware that Gulley & Co owes its success to and depends for it's future on the continued support, goodwill, hard work and pulling together of you as its staff. The unveiling of this plaque is as much homage to the fruits of your years here as is it the twenty-five years it celebrates. (*Pause.*) Did it go something like that?

DEBBIE: More or less.

DAVE: For he's a jolly good fellow and so say all of us.

DEBBIE: We can go home early today.

DAVE: I know. Special treat for a special day. Special evening – tonight . . .

DEBBIE: You're going to do it, ain't yah?

DAVE: Do what?

DEBBIE: You know what.

DAVE: Serving drinks at the party? Who me? Polishing the glasses and putting in the ice – are you serious? Taking round the sherry on a tray, stacking the empties away – what do you take me for? That'd be capitulation, caving in – giving way, bottling out. After everything I've said, that'd be . . .

DEBBIE: Hypocritical.

DAVE: Right.

DEBBIE: You're doing it though, ain't ya?

DAVE: Yeah.

DEBBIE: Why?

DAVE: Lawrence doesn't need many more excuses to give me the push.

DEBBIE: He wouldn't do that.

DAVE: Not so crudely, no. But he'd call me into his office and 'suggest' that I might be happier working somewhere else, somewhere I could fit in better, where I might find 'fewer problems' to the ones I seem to be having here. It would be to our mutual interests and as he'd tactfully point out – it would be a much more satisfactory arrangement all round if I resigned rather than them having to dismiss me. That would then make life very difficult for me, future employment prospects and all that, he'd say. A stain on my *curriculum vitae,* he'd say. And I'd have Hobson's choice.

DEBBIE: I got the veiled threats and nudge-nudge blackmail as well.

DAVE: Yeah, but he didn't catch you hiding in a cupboard did he – wearing inappropriate clothes? And you didn't jump out on him and burst two balloons in his face did ya? (*Pause.*) I'm making amends, as they say.

DEBBIE: By turning up tonight with a tea towel over your arm?

DAVE: All those 'positive' words he used to try and make our ears burn – co-operation, trust, interest and commitment – like he was calling out bingo numbers – whether he meant it or not it doesn't matter . . . they'll be applying to me tonight won't they? Part of the team . . . acting in the right spirit . . . (*Pause.*) Politics innit? (*Self-mocking.*) Clever, shrewd old me. Talk about calculating eh? Talk about knowing when to compromise. (*Turning to self-disgust.*) Playing safe – I'm good at that as well. It's my best thing. I'm a fucking expert. Have you noticed?

DEBBIE: Perhaps it's more to do with knowing which side you're bread's buttered.

DAVE: Oh I know all about that all right – I keep being told don't I? I'm one of the fortunate few – one of the bright young sparks with the chance to get on. (*He laughs.*) Get on, that's what all the 'O' levels were for – getting on. Not clever enough for university, but clever enough to punch holes in files and address envelopes. Working-class boy – working hard to better himself. Leaves school with certificates under arm – apply for suitable positions that reflect my academic standards. End up here. Stockbroker's. In the City. Mum and Dad are very proud. Bought me a pocket calculator when I joined. Their son's done well. Won't ever have to come home covered in shit and aches and pains. Won't wind up like the other kids round here – nicking cars, being put away and kiting and no future. Different to them. I'm one of the lucky ones and I should be grateful.

DEBBIE: It's like Lawrence said – this is England, 1982, and you've got three million reasons for being grateful.

DAVE: I know – and I think I grew up with 10,000 of 'em. Lose those mates anyway, ones you grew up with. Don't feel the same anymore. What they do – it's not the same world as this. Avoid the pubs they go in. Can't talk.

DEBBIE: I still go out with the same girls I knew when I was twelve. You don't have to become something else.

DAVE: No, but you're expected to. It's the mark of success – to get introduced to the nicer class of people and climb on. That's what doing well is supposed to mean innit – shrugging off the 'stink' of your background. Move out of the East End, buy a little house in Billericay, start calling egg and bacon flan quiche lorraine, start filling up shelves with books you'll never read, start trying. Get out and get a mortgage, get promoted, get your own four drawer filing cabinet, get a plant for it . . . the human touch. Become like Lawrence or try to become like him, like the people you despise. That's getting on (*Pause.*) Education for mediocrity . . . if you're lucky. (*Pause.*) Still – you can always ring up Dial a Disc when you get bored, can't ya?

DEBBIE: Or think about the weekends. At least working here gives you the freedom to go and get drunk on Pernod and lemonade at Benjy's or Cheeks and have a laugh and get a cab home or get taken home sometimes. Friday night. Saturday night. Some people can't afford fun anymore – at least I can. Once or twice a week anyway. I'm not saying it's enough cos it ain't – I'd like to try working abroad for a couple of months, give me the chance to learn another language as well, y'know – that's if me Mum wouldn't miss me money too much. Anyway, I don't think I'll have to worry too much about your quiche lorraine – not while people like Lawrence think I'm nothing more than two boobs in a blouse. At the moment, all it can be is a means to an end. This.

DAVE: A weekend.

DEBBIE: Maybe. I can make choices and that's not bad, y'know. Some of the girls I did grow up with – who've never had a job – they get pregnant so they'll have something. Compared to them I'm lucky cos I can go to clubs and have a fortnight in Benidorm. (*Pause.*) Anyway I hope you have a nice time tonight. Behave yourself.

DAVE: What d'you expect me to do? I think I'm always going to behave meself – I'm a clerk and I think I've got piss in me veins now.

She goes.
DAVE is left alone.

Scene Eight

That evening. Darkness. We hear someone crashing through the door of the basement. Lights switched on. It is DAVE. He is breathless – holding a gift-wrapped package, wearing a bar steward's jacket. He is half-drunk. He locks the door. Having done that, he unwraps the package with great care. It is a carriage clock.

DAVE: Handsome! Fucking handsome! (*He puts it on the desk, surveying his prize.*) Nice one! Spoils of war! (*Walking round it.*) The not so meek shall inherit the carriage clock. I wonder how much you cost then? Got to be more than we collected. Must have been a top-up,

someone putting their hand in their wallet! Lawrence! Kicks!

A voice from outside.

David, are you in there?

DAVE: No, I ain't in here. No one's in here. It's empty. Deserted.

LAWRENCE: Can you please tell me what's going on?

DAVE: I'm admiring this clock here. It's a very nice clock. What a lovely presentation gift for Mr Gulley – I bet he's thrilled with it. More like *was* thrilled with it.

LAWRENCE: Look – I don't know what you think you're hoping to achieve with this buffoonery . . .

DAVE: Buffoonery! Stroll on Lawrence – you make me sound like Billy Bunter.

LAWRENCE: You'll be in bloody deep water if you don't come out.

DAVE (*mimicking*): 'You'll be in bloody deep water if you don't come out.' I (*Pause.*) I ain't coming out and you ain't getting in. You're the big bad wolf, Lawrence. You always have been. And what does the big bad wolf say?

LAWRENCE: You're drunk you little bastard.

DAVE: No, he don't say that. (*Pause.*) Gulley's present is going to have to get swept up with a dustpan and brush if you don't tell me what the big bad wolf says. Little pieces. Cross my heart. (*Pause.*) I'll fucking do it! Come on, Lawrence, what does he say? (*Pause.*) I'm waiting! (*Pause.*)

LAWRENCE: I'll huff and I'll puff and I'll blow your house down.

DAVE (*laughing*): Not by the hairs on your chinny chin chin!

LAWRENCE: Let's be adult about this, David. Come on – stop playing the fool and hand over the clock. You're holding up the presentation – everybody's waiting.

DAVE: I know. Fucking great, ain't it? Bet it's one long pregnant pause up there. Bet the collective stiff upper lip is starting to quiver.

LAWRENCE: It is a little embarrassing to

have nothing to present at the presentation . . . You've succeeded in causing some awkward moments at least. Now let's call it a day OK? I'm quite prepared to let this one go as a bit of high spirits, a case of someone a little the worse for wear. I'll overlook the fact that you should have been serving the drinks not swallowing them if you'll just come out with the gift and let the evening proceed as it should.

DAVE: Going to kindly dispense your justice and mercy are you? You're only saying all that cos you're desperate. Be a different story when it's in your hands.

LAWRENCE: You're not being fair.

DAVE: Funny innit – that's what Debbie said to you the other day. Deeply ironic that is. I bet you appreciate the deep irony of that, don't you Mr Lawrence? (*Pause.*) Finders keepers, losers weepers.

LAWRENCE (*furious*): You'll be out of this firm so fast you're arse won't touch the ground, Shell!

DAVE: Temper, temper Mr Lawrence. That's not very nice is it? But I'm quite prepared to overlook that as a bit of high spirits. I'll let that one go as a bit of rash behaviour. (*Pause.*) I bet you're sweating out there. I hope I haven't spoilt the party, I hope this doesn't become a black day in the history of Gulley & Co. And if it does, make sure they spell my name right. I know you're always telling me to co-operate Mr L., but I've got to stop the piss flowing through my veins, you know. I'm sorry I'm not acting in the right spirit, I'm sorry I'm not being part of the team . . . I've just been sent off for a bad foul. Has this damaged my prospects Mr L? My future in the firm, my house in Billericay, my quiche lorraine, my four drawer filing cabinet?

LAWRENCE: I'm afraid I don't understand a word you're saying.

DAVE: I didn't think you would.

LAWRENCE: Is there something you want to talk about? Some problem about work you want to discuss? I'm willing to listen.

DAVE: You're listening now fat arse – you've got no choice. You're squirming now. You called me a psychopath before. You was wrong, I'm a kleptomaniac – and I've nicked the centrepiece of the

evening, ain't I? You took the piss out of me – ever so dryly, ever so I'm in control, ever so you're just shit on my shoe and I scrape you off by the kerb. So fucking sure of yourself – you was enjoying watching me gulp and stammer – playing with me – like pulling the wings off a butterfly. I'm playing now and it's my game.

LAWRENCE: If you wanted to vent your spleen on me you could at least have done it in a less cowardly fashion than this.

DAVE: What – man to man? Or clerk to departmental head. No, I like it better this way – tactics of warfare diplomacy – negotiate from a position of strength.

LAWRENCE: Negotiate what?

DAVE: I want . . . I want in return for handing over this clock . . . I want relief from my . . . profound disappointment and disillusionment, and I want relief from my piles as well.

LAWRENCE: You're behaving like a child who can't get his own way. All it amounts to is foot stamping. Over what? Some unexplained, mysterious bloody grievance of yours? (*Pause.*) Let me in and we'll sort it out – would you like to do more figure work, is that it?

DAVE: You crack me up, I tell ya!

LAWRENCE: You could at least let me in.

DAVE: You don't know the password.

LAWRENCE: That clock is worth quite a lot of money, you know. Your friends and colleagues contributed out of their own pockets to enable that to be bought. It's an act of vandalism against them as much as anyone else.

DAVE: But they wouldn't have been taking it home with 'em and putting it on their mantlepieces, would they? Anyway don't preach to me – I helped do the fucking collection for it remember?

LAWRENCE: Please don't do anything stupid.

DAVE: What – like let you in? Repeat the password and I'll let you in.

LAWRENCE: What password?

DAVE: Fleshy buttocks. That's the password.

LAWRENCE: I hope you've got another

fucking job lined up, Shell! This gratuitious display . . .

DAVE *picks up a cup and throws it at the door. It smashes.*

LAWRENCE: Jesus Christ David! What the fucking hell d'you think you're playing at? If that was Mr Gulley's presentation gift . . .

DAVE: It will be the next time – unless you give me the password.

LAWRENCE: You promise to let me in?

DAVE: *Dictum meum pactum.* My word is my bond, as we say in the Stock Exchange.

LAWRENCE: D'you want this accompanied by a little dance or what?

DAVE: Just the password, please.

LAWRENCE: I want an assurance that the clock is all right.

DAVE: I just told you. Now get on with it – the password. Then I'll open up and face you man to man – I'd rather see you sweating in the flesh anyway. Watch you being anxious as fuck, vulnerable. Chance of a lifetime.

LAWRENCE: So you'll let me in if I give you this . . . password?

DAVE: You catch on fast. You'll do well here if you show the right attitude. (*Pause.*) C'mon spit it out.

LAWRENCE: OK. (*Pause.*) The password is . . . fleshy buttocks.

DAVE: Wrong.

LAWRENCE: You promised me!

DAVE *picks up the clock and goes to open the door. He moves back as* LAWRENCE *comes in.*

DAVE: Keep your distance or this'll slip through me fingers.

LAWRENCE: I really expected something better from you, David.

DAVE: I know what you expect. You expect people to fit it. Be reassuringly pleasant and mediocre and marginal. Plod on, play the game, play the white man. Be a good sport. A good bloke. Straight as a die. Never grumbles, never asks why. Moderation and no cause for offence. Do my best. Happy to be rewarded by . . . promises of progress within the firm. Just let me have my own lawn and the time to water it. Values of the suburban nonentities. I don't need 'em. They're paper thin.

LAWRENCE: Your self-conscious 'gesture of defiance' will be thought of as nothing more than the antics of a drunk. A tantrum thrown under the influence of alcohol. You'll think so too when you wake up in the morning.

DAVE: Tell me mates about this . . . they'll be rolled up.

LAWRENCE: Rebel without a job.

DAVE: Be the talk of the firm tomorrow. And for weeks afterwards. What I've done tonight.

LAWRENCE: It won't be with admiration.

DAVE: You got the message. All of you.

LAWRENCE: D'you think a company like this is interested in or bothered by the dissatisfactions and frustrations of one junior clerk? Don't overestimate yourself. The noise and fuss you make is about as significant as a piss in the ocean. Trying to take us on by pulling this kind of stunt will get you nothing but your P45 thrust in your hand and a finger pointing to the door. We haven't got the time or the inclination to put up with your self-indulgence.

DAVE: Smash . . . smash this I will!

LAWRENCE: If you'd been serious you'd have done it ten minutes ago. Let's get this back upstairs and put an end to this little drama. Besides you don't want to get done by the police for theft and criminal damage do you?

DAVE: You're not worth it.

LAWRENCE *takes the clock. As he leaves:*

You're not worth it! (*Shouting out still –* LAWRENCE *has gone.*) I fucking showed 'em . . . put the cat among the rats didn't I? Whatever next – a trade union? What's the password – big bad wolf. Happy birthday Gulley & Co from a well wisher. One of the lucky ones. Wait till Debbie hears about this. I didn't behave meself.

Scene Nine

Next morning. LAWRENCE, TIMOTHY *and*
JOE *are in the basement.*

LAWRENCE: Yes, it's very definitely a
case of the morning after the night before,
up there and it doesn't look at all decent.
If you could go and get it into some
recognisable orderly state it'd be a bonus.

DEBBIE *enters, taking off her coat.*

LAWRENCE: Ah – the return of the
prodigal daughter.

DEBBIE: Beg your pardon?

LAWRENCE: We were just talking about
what fun the party turned out to be last
night. Pity you couldn't be there.

DEBBIE: Yeah . . . shame really.

TIMOTHY: But not exactly a tragedy.

DEBBIE: Well, at least Timothy was here
to be the life and soul of it.

JOE: There was chicken legs left over – so
we took 'em home.

DEBBIE: Eventful as well then.

JOE: Eh?

DEBBIE: The party. What with chicken
legs being taken home and everything.
(*Pause.*) A lot happening, sort of thing.

LAWRENCE: Facetious this morning
aren't we, Debbie? (*Pause.*) Yes, apart
from one slight technical hitch, it went off
very well, I thought.

Pause.

DEBBIE: Where's Dave?

TIMOTHY: Great timing you've got.
(*Laughing.*)

LAWRENCE: David is no longer with us.

DEBBIE: What d'you mean?

LAWRENCE: David was the slight
technical hitch last night. (*Pause.*) It was
decided that it would be in his best
interests and ours too if he . . . resigned. It
wasn't felt appropriate in the
circumstances to worry about one
month's notice. (*Pause.*) He's not coming
back.

DEBBIE: What did he do?

LAWRENCE: There was an incident . . .
concerning the presentation gift for Mr
Gulley.

JOE: He ran away with it. Headcase, eh? I
couldn't believe it.

LAWRENCE (*to* JOE): Nice to know you
want to be my spokesman. If I remember
rightly you and Timothy have got a date
with the conference room, rearranged
furniture and empty cases of wines and
spirits. I'll be up in due course to see how
you're coping . . .

TIM *and* JOE *go.*
Pause.

Yes, he did run away with it. Rather like
the dish did with the spoon. But he didn't
go far, his little outburst fizzled out and
after a short wait Mr Gulley became the
smiling recipient of a very impressive
carriage clock which was the plan all
along, as you know.

DEBBIE: Happy ending, sort of thing.

LAWRENCE: Great rejoicing throughout
the land. (*Pause.*) He was a good friend of
yours wasn't he?

DEBBIE: I liked him, a lot. We had things
in common.

LAWRENCE: A closer than average pair,
eh? (*Pause.*) Yes, I can certainly see that
now. (*Pause.*) A pair with a lot of
potential. A good pair, potentially. Still,
I'm sure you've been told that before.
(*Pause.*) About your potential.

DEBBIE: I could trust Dave. And he
respected me. That's ever so important,
don't you think – trust and respect? If you
can't trust someone and you feel they
don't respect you – it's a bit hopeless
innit? A waste of time

LAWRENCE: Oh I agree. A hundred per
cent. That's what friendship's all about.
And I think it's always good to have a
shoulder to lean on, someone to confide
in and seek advice from, a crutch in times
of crisis. If David gave you that kind of
support, you were very lucky indeed.
And if you do feel in the future that from
time to time, you'd like a crutch to lean on
– you'll always be free to lean on mine. I
wouldn't mind in the least. As your
departmental head, that's partly what I'm
here for. And what with your potential
and my crutch or vice-versa even – that's
the making of a great team, don't you
think?

DEBBIE: I think a lot of the time it's much better to be independent, you know? To steer clear of other people's good intentions and attentions. Otherwise, it can cause more trouble than you might have already got.

LAWRENCE: Perhaps you're right. You look to me like the kind of girl who doesn't really need any support.

DEBBIE: As I was just saying about trouble – I'm not the kind of girl who really needs it (*Pause.*) or wants to cause it. Not unless I have to.

LAWRENCE: Yes, I appreciate the position you take. Or to be more accurate, I'd like to appreciate the position you take.

Pause.

DEBBIE: You're quite persuasive, ain't ya? I think you're wearing my resistance down to be honest.

LAWRENCE: Is that such a bad thing?

DEBBIE: Perhaps not. What's your first name Mr Lawrence?

LAWRENCE: Clive.

DEBBIE: I know you're married and that . . .

LAWRENCE: Does it bother you?

DEBBIE: No – I was just going to say – I don't mind.

LAWRENCE: Good – neither do I.

DEBBIE: I'm quite realistic about these kinds of situations.

LAWRENCE: Glad to hear it.

DEBBIE: Some girls wouldn't want to know about getting involved with a married bloke. But if you want to take me out and spend a lot of money on me – a girl who's never had much . . . I'd be silly to turn the chance down. I'm old enough to know what I want – and what you want, come to that.

LAWRENCE: Right . . .

She pulls his wig off.

Bitch!

DEBBIE: That was for Dave as well. I told you we had things in common.

LAWRENCE: Fucking bitch! You'll have

unemployment in common as well now – that's your fucking lot! Out on your arse girl and no mistake!

DEBBIE: I'm going to work in a travel agent's. I'll have more opportunities for travel. I've been offered a job. There aren't many left anymore but I'm one of the lucky ones. (*Pause.*) That's why I've been facetious this morning.

During this, JOE *and* TIM *enter unseen by* LAWRENCE.

LAWRENCE: I'll sue you for assault if I can! If it's at all possible I fucking will! I mean it! I'll make you even more of a loser than you are already – I'll pull those other two toe-rags in as witnesses. They'll do just what they're told because they think the firm can pull them up by their shoddy little bootlaces. But they'll find out eventually that they didn't go to quite the right schools and don't make quite the right vowel sounds to really get anywhere in this wonderful company. But they'll help me sort you out before they do.

JOE: Where's your hair gone Mr Lawrence?